Marketing for Cultural Organisations

2nd edition

ABOUT THE AUTHOR

Dr Bonita M. Kolb currently teaches marketing at Lycoming College in Pennsylvania. She also teaches in the graduate programmes at the Pratt Institute in New York and the Sibelius Academy in Helsinki. She has conducted marketing research with cultural institutions in both the US and Europe such as the Brooklyn Museum of Art, Opera Ebony, the London Philharmonic Orchestra, BBC Proms and Wigmore Hall.

Marketing for Cultural Organisations

2nd edition

*New Strategies for Attracting Audiences
to Classical Music, Dance, Museums,
Theatre & Opera*

Bonita M. Kolb

THOMSON

Marketing for Cultural Organisations

Copyright © Bonita M. Kolb 2005

The Thomson logo is a registered trademark used herein under licence.

For more information, contact Thomson Learning, High Holborn House,
50–51 Bedford Row, London WC1R 4LR or visit us on the World Wide Web at:
http://www.thomsonlearning.co.uk

British Library Cataloguing-in-Publication Data
A catalogue record for this book is available from the British Library

ISBN 1-84480-213-2

First Edition published in 1999 by Oak Tree Press, Cork, Ireland
Published in 2005 by Thomson Learning

Typeset by LaserScript, Mitcham, Surrey

Printed in Croatia by Zrinski d.d.

CONTENTS

WORKSHEETS

PREFACE

Why a book on marketing for cultural organisations? After all, haven't cultural organisations already learned all they need to know about marketing?

Cultural organisations have been familiar with marketing theory for the last 30 years. Over this time period, they have become more skilled in the use of marketing skills and tools. What they have not done is to adopt the marketing concept that states marketing is not about skills and tools but rather about building a relationship between the organisation and the customer. This relationship must be built between equals and is based on the needs of the customer. Unfortunately some cultural organisations have wrongly felt that this approach was counter to their mission.

In the past, cultural organisations could afford this belief because they were protected from the harsh realities of the marketplace by public subsidies. However, as the subsidies decreased, cultural organisations have found that they need to learn more about marketing skills so they can attract an audience that is increasingly difficult to find.

Since this book was first published, a second phenomenon – societal changes – has increased the importance of cultural organisations revisiting their attitude toward marketing. This is because societal changes have resulted in a new type of customer: the culture consumer. Culture consumers owe no allegiance to any particular art form, or even to art in general. They want a cultural experience, but only if it also entertains. Furthermore, because they are constantly bombarded with media messages, cultural organisations must use promotion in new and different ways.

This book will help practitioners in both large and small cultural organisations to apply the marketing concept. The premise of this book is that this new approach can be done while still remaining true to the organisational mission. The book focuses on those aspects of marketing most related to the challenges currently facing cultural organisations, including determining their market segment and promoting their cultural product as a packaged event.

The book will also be valuable, used alone or as a supplemental text, for students who are studying arts management. It could also be used in the teaching of standard marketing classes, as the blurring of the distinction between the non-profit and for-profit worlds, especially in creative industries, makes it increasingly likely that the challenges discussed in the book will be faced by a wide range of students.

Throughout the book, examples are provided of how cultural organisations have successfully applied marketing strategy. It is hoped that those working in cultural organisations will be inspired to also meet the new challenges with new ideas. The worksheets at the end of each chapter can be used by students or practitioners to develop their own marketing plan.

Marketing is a process and the chapters are arranged to guide you through this process. The first chapter examines the history and development of cultural organisations, including how they have changed and their current situation they face. Emphasis is placed on the changing social environment in which cultural organisations must now function. These changes have resulted in new challenges for all cultural organisations.

The second chapter examines in detail how the manner in which the public views culture has changed. The blurring of the distinction between high and popular culture, the demand by the audience to be entertained, and the increase in knowledge of world culture has dramatically changed the ability of the cultural organisation to dictate to their audience their own definition of art and the appropriate manner in which it should be presented. The views of Adorno, Gans and Bourdieu are discussed.

Chapter Three discusses the media audience model proposed by Abercrombie and Longhurst and how it can be adapted to better understand cultural audiences. Particular attention is given to the concept of the culture consumer. This chapter also discusses how attendance patterns are affected by generational value shifts.

Chapter Four focuses on the development of marketing theory and its use in both corporate businesses and non-profit cultural institutions. The difference between the production, sales and market approach to the marketing function is examined.

Chapter Five examines consumer motivation and how knowledge of the purchase process and the benefits sought by consumers can help cultural organisations design a marketing strategy. Using market segmentation in audience development is the focus of **Chapter Six**. A special focus is given in this chapter to targeting cultural tourists. Audience research is discussed in **Chapter Seven**, with emphasis on how small cultural organisations can effectively use qualitative techniques.

Chapter Eight discusses the cultural product, its features, benefits and distribution. It explains how culture can be packaged as a product that provides multiple benefits to consumers. **Chapter Nine** discusses the impact that non-profit status and the resulting pressure to raise funds has on cultural organisations. Different pricing concepts, and their use by non-profits, are considered.

The final chapter, **Chapter Ten**, provides information on promoting the cultural product using advertising, sales incentives, personal selling, public relations and direct marketing.

After each chapter worksheets are provided. These worksheets use a question and answer format to encourage readers who are practitioners or postgraduate students to apply the concepts they have learned to their own organisation. If a post-graduate student is currently unemployed, they can chose a cultural organisation for whom they are interested in working and use the worksheets completion as a networking opportunity.

Teachers using the book for undergraduates can use these worksheets as the basis for a semester-long written project. The student can choose a cultural organisation in which they are interested. They then can complete the worksheets based on both library research and interviews with organisational personnel. At the end of the semester, a written marketing plan can be handed into the teacher and provided to the organisation.

The examples that are presented throughout the book are placed near relevant marketing information. These examples can be either used as a basis for classroom discussion or be assigned to students to conduct additional research on the organisation or topic.

While the management and purpose of cultural organisations tends to vary to some extent in different countries, there is still an immediately recognisable similarity across national borders as to purpose of the product and the intended audience. The ambience of a museum may vary from the US to Japan but there is no confusion as to the fact that both are museums. The same can be said of theatre, classical music, opera and dance. For this reason, the marketing information in this book can be applied across national boundaries.

Chapter One

NEW MARKETING CHALLENGES

The world was a very different place in the 1970s when the field of arts marketing was popularised. What has changed? Since then, the external societal environment in which cultural organisations exist has changed dramatically. The changes include new employment patterns, globalisation, increase in the frequency of marketing messages, the blurring of the boundary between popular and high art and increased funding pressures.

SOCIETAL CHANGES

For example, today life is more stressful than a generation ago. People are working harder for longer hours, as industries strive to compete in a global marketplace (Putnam, 2001). People live farther from work and face long commutes at the end of the workday. Single parents and working women face a double challenge of meeting both work and family responsibilities. As a result, there are fewer hours and less energy for leisure activities. When there is an opportunity for leisure, although people may still want to experience art, they understandably also want to be entertained.

The world has also become smaller. Technology has enabled people to experience music and visual arts from around the world with a click of their mouse. Because the cost of travel has declined, more people have direct experience with different cultures. As a result, they no longer automatically view other cultures as "foreign". Indeed, increased immigration means that these formerly "foreign" cultures may be encountered down the street.

At the same time that life has become more stressful and culturally complex, people are faced with an increasing barrage of marketing messages regarding leisure activities (Cappo, 2003).

This promotional overload results in people tuning out advertising, which has increased the difficulty of successful promotion. The days when a well-designed brochure or advertisement was sufficient have ended. Cultural organisations must be as creative in their promotions as they are in their art.

The very nature of the competition faced by cultural organisations has changed. Where formerly they considered other organisations with similar art forms as their competition, they must now broaden their view. This is because the once distinct worlds of high culture *versus* popular culture and national culture *versus* foreign culture have now blended. As a result, cultural organisations and entertainment companies with both national and ethnic offerings are competing for the limited time and attention of the same consumer.

To further complicate the situation, over the last two decades, along with government funding cutbacks, there has been a decline in the number of the traditional patrons of high culture willing to support the arts out of a love of art or a sense of responsibility. This has strained the financial resources of many cultural organisations and increased the need to focus on ticket revenue.

The Good News

Fortunately, there is good news. While many new challenges must be faced by those marketing the arts, a new potential audience is obtainable. This new audience, which can be called cultural consumers, are willing to attend – if they are invited to do so with the right product and promotional message. These new consumers of culture are interested in the arts, but also insist on being entertained. They do not have a reverence for high art or an interest only in Western culture. They may attend a rock concert one night, and the opera the next. They may enjoy a Mozart concert while watching a laser light show in a Planetarium and also enjoy listening to Tibetan chanting in a traditional concert hall.

The Evolving Purpose of the Museum

How many purposes can a museum have? At first, museums were formed to both give pleasure and to educate. A more recent purpose has been to provide an opportunity for spiritual uplift. Today museums try to combine a bit of all three elements and as a result have become a new public space for the community.

But how do you combine all three elements and still satisfy the purists who only come for the art? The J. Paul Getty Museum in Los Angeles used focus groups to tell them how to do it differently. The result is more information on the walls so that those new to art can easily enjoy what they see. For those who want education, there are computers that provide additional information. To help the visitor engage with what they are seeing, there are laminated cards that ask challenging questions. And, if they need to ponder the meaning of the art, there are now comfortable chairs instead of hard benches.

In fact, the Museum's mission statement states that its purpose is not only to educate but also to "delight" and "inspire".

Source: Keates, 1999; Getty, 2004.

DEVELOPING A MARKETING PLAN

As a result of these societal changes and the resulting change in consumer behaviour, cultural organisations must come to a new understanding of how culture is marketed and consumed as a product. A special type of product, but a product nevertheless. They must also understand how consumers make choices between cultural products based on their internal needs not on external distinctions between types of culture. Cultural organisations now need to know more than just the basics of marketing. They need to know how to use the marketing concept to develop a marketing plan, that uses new product and promotional strategies to successfully target culture consumers.

In the process of developing a marketing plan, the cultural organisation will be forced to examine critically the external environmental forces that affect their ability to attract an audience. These forces include new competition for consumers' time and money. This competition may be from other cultural organisations or from popular cultural establishments. They also must examine changes in community preferences. The popularity of different art forms changes in the same way as the popularity of other types of products. They must consider changes in funding. A decrease in funding will increase pressure to develop the audience so as to improve revenue. Technological changes can force cultural organisations to use more technology because of public expectations. The economic situation also affects the cultural organisation. If the economy is in difficulty, people will have less money to spend, making pricing an issue.

Along with a statement of organisational mission, this process of examining external forces that affect the cultural organisation is the first step in developing a marketing plan. The plan is a roadmap of the steps involved in reaching the goal of an effective marketing strategy. But it also benefits an organisation in other ways. A marketing plan can help to explain to the organisation why and how it should spend money on marketing. A marketing plan can also help in assigning responsibility for different tasks and assist in integrating new employees into the organisation.

Additional steps in developing a marketing plan include an analysis of the organisation's competitors. After which the cultural organisation must examine their current audience's motivation for attendance. The next step is to target a new audience and plan the research needed to determine the benefits they desire. The major task then faced by the cultural organisation is to consider how they can adapt their product, pricing and distribution to provide these benefits, while at the same time remaining true to their own unique organisational mission. Only then will they be able to design a promotional campaign that targets the right people with the right message.

Components of a Marketing Plan

1. Statement of Organisational Mission
↓
2. Environmental Analysis
↓
3. Competitor Analysis
↓
4. Understanding Buyer Motivation
↓
5. Segmentation
↓
6. Research Plan
↓
7. Product Analysis
↓
8. Distribution Analysis
↓
9. Pricing Options
↓
10. Promotional Plan

New Marketing Strategies

To attract the cultural consumer it is important for organisations to include new creative marketing strategies in their marketing plan. These strategies include packaging a cultural product as an event that combines both culture and entertainment. Such packaged events may involve collaboration between different cultural organisations, combine high and popular culture or use new distribution systems for delivering culture to customers. In addition, the packaged event might be promoted by both cultural organisations and businesses as a means of building community or attracting tourists. These events will still meet the mission of enriching lives by increasing exposure to the arts and at the same time, will provide a complete package of benefits that motivate consumers to attend. Many examples of such strategies are provided throughout this book.

The End of Cultural Distinctions and Hierarchy

Throughout this book, the familiar distinctions between high art and popular culture will be challenged. Also questioned will be the traditional hierarchy of a paternal organisation informing a submissive audience what they should consume. When developing marketing strategies, it is becoming increasingly difficult to justify the old distinction between "high" art and "popular" culture (Staniszewski, 1995). But it is also becoming less important as more people, unconcerned with value judgements regarding the relative worth of each, consume both. This disregard for the historical distinction between types of cultural products results from changes in the social structure of society and the continuing success of commercial popular culture (DiMaggio, 2000).

It's Not Your Grandmother's Orchestra

The Fort Wayne Philharmonic (Texas) promotes concerts to take advantage of the MTV Unplugged phenomena. A look at their website shows a picture of musicians looking very trendy with the tag line "Lose the Attitude. Get Unplugged".

The orchestra is described as: "Loud. Hard. Fast. The Original. This isn't a polite night at the concert hall. Hear the classical pieces that give the orchestra a workout and make the audience leap to their feet with applause. Violin bows will be flying. Percussion mallets will be pounding. And you will experience the famous classical pieces that defined intensity and passion in music."

Source: Fort Wayne Philharmonic, 2004.

Even using the word "art" to describe an object or event is problematic, as it immediately implies that a value judgement is being made. Under the old definition, this judgement is necessary to determine whether the object or event deserves to be placed in an art institution. There is, of course, a place for this value judgement between worthy art and commercial popular culture, as long as it is understood that the judgement is being made by humans – not by divine intervention – and is subject to change over time.

It is now accepted that marketing strategy can be of use to those involved in presenting all types of culture including high, popular, local, ethnic and world. However it is necessary for cultural organisations to do more than just learn marketing techniques. Basic to marketing theory is the concept that the customer is an equal partner in the exchange of money for goods. Cultural organisations have historically had a top down approach of "we know what is best for you". For marketing to be successful they must now realign their organisation to one of equal partnership, where they take the customers' needs and desires seriously. This new relationship can be visualised as a triangle with the cultural organisation and the audience sharing equal importance and in communication with each other.

Relationship Between Product, Organisation and Audience

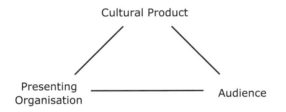

WHAT IS A CULTURAL ORGANISATION?

The word *art* is often paired with the word *institution*. Looking in the thesaurus, a synonym for art is *aptitude* and a synonym for institution is *place*. So an art institution can be defined as a place that contains aptitude of the highest level or as a temple to artistic achievement – which is how it is often viewed by the public. The problem with this definition is that it separates art from the everyday world in which people live.

This book uses the term "cultural organisation" instead of "art institution" for a reason. Cultural organisations should think of themselves as members of their communities. They should view their art as something they wish to share, rather than impose from above. For this reason instead of the word *art*, the word *culture* is used, as it applies in a broad sense to all events or objects created by a society to communicate certain cultural values.

Instead of the word *institution*, the word *organisation* is used. An institution is a place, but organisations are defined as groups of people. Although the people who make up the organisation may work in a building, it should not fine them. In fact, to be an organisation does not require a building. The organisation may work out of another public or private institution, out of cyberspace or from the back of a van.

Definition of Cultural Organisation

Old Definition

Art : Aptitude + Institution : Place = Aptitude Place

New Definition

Culture : Society's Events/Objects + Organisation : People = Object/Event People

In addition, the familiar distinction between the non-profit world of high culture and the for-profit world of popular culture is also breaking down. While non-profit cultural organisations now must worry about selling a product, and therefore hire marketing professionals, for-profit companies which produce popular culture are now able to attract talented artists to work for them. For-profit multimedia, design and entertainment companies are particularly seen as legitimate users of artistic talent.

The Development of Cultural Organisations

If the urge to communicate and create is innate to the human spirit, then there have always been artists. However the freedom for an individual to create unencumbered by the need to sell the work to obtain the money needed for everyday existence is a modern development. The necessity to provide the basics of survival was paramount and the art that was created needed to have some social purpose to justify its existence. There was simply no resources or energy to spare for art for art's sake.

However when society organised itself into the ruled and the rulers, the rulers then had the money and time to have artistic objects created just for them. Many of these objects had spiritual significance, and this use of art for religious purposes was continued after the founding of the Christian church. For much of history, only the royal rulers and the church had the wealth to patronise the arts. This was true during the Middle Ages, when artists created objects of worship for the church and objects of pleasure for royal houses. The art for both groups was also a symbol of status.

As the wealth of society developed in Europe during the Renaissance, the patronage of the arts began to expand and the great merchant families had the wealth to join royalty and the church in playing a critical role in supporting individual artists. With the growing importance of commerce, these newly wealthy merchants began to patronise artists (Sweetman, 1998). The art performance or object was purchased to fill newly found leisure time or as possessions to adorn the home. These merchants were not individually wealthy enough to support an artist, but, through many of them purchasing art, artists were now able to survive. Patronage by either a royal individual, church or merchant provided the artist with economic support. In exchange, it was considered the artist's duty to provide art that appealed to the taste of the patron. The artist's individual artistic vision was considered of secondary importance, if it was considered at all.

In the 18th century, there was a change in the way society viewed the artist. Rather than being seen merely as a craftsman whose skill was used as a means to glorify others, European society began to treat the artist as a special category of person entitled to create art based on their own personal vision.

The growth in the wealth and power of towns and cities resulted in civil governments taking on the burden of supporting artists, which was formerly the responsibility of the court, church and merchant family. In fact cities often competed with each other to obtain the services of the most famous artist in a manner similar to the way modern cities court football teams.

However, in more recent times, rather than support the artist directly, the city and wealthy tradesmen now fund the organisation sponsoring the artist or presenting the art form. Rather than artists being supported by religious or royal patrons, or their being dependent upon the whims of merchants, the idea of a professionally managed institution that supports the artist was invented (Björkegren, 1996). These cultural organisations have supplanted the patron of the past. The modern arrangement is for the cultural organisation to be supported by public funding and staffed by people who are not artists, but closely believe in the vision of the artist. By identifying with the artist and art form, they consciously create a different type of management environment in the cultural institution than that which would prevail in a for-profit organisation.

Museum Shops: Commerce and Culture

"Museums have invested considerable time, money and space in shops. Retail workers have injected enterprise and user-friendliness, branded goods have been introduced and product licensing is being developed. Commerce and culture seem to be united: the museum benefits from sales, and the visitor benefits from the integrity of the museum which acts as guarantor and arbiter of quality ... . Museum shops have evolved from demanding but dependent cuckoos into autonomous entities ... .

One indignant Friend of the Victoria & Albert Museum replied to her questionnaire: 'No one goes to a museum in order to shop.'

Oh yes they do."

And now the V&A has its own online Netalogue where you can buy all the museum gift items and send free e-cards without coming to the museum. Why? It makes money, keeps the museum's name in front of the public and builds a relationship that encourages repeat visits.

Source: Norris, 1997; Vandashop, 2004.

Cultural Management

Traditionally, the management of cultural organisations has been viewed as safely separate and distinct from other types of business organisations. As a result of this belief, those working in cultural organisations did not feel they needed to manage their organisations as businesses. It was assumed that different rules would apply to the management of cultural organisations – just as different rules applied to artists. They both would be protected from the distasteful business of making a living, justifying what they were doing and providing a product pleasing to the mass public.

It was only during the 1970s that cultural organisations came to the widespread realisation that, if there was to be sufficient attendance, it would be necessary to market their art to the public (Heilbrun and Gray, 2001). As a result, cultural organisations created marketing departments. At first, the marketing strategy created by these departments was to adopt standard business promotional practices. They started to market by simply placing advertisements that communicated a broad marketing message on the availability of the art that was being provided.

They could hardly do more. Cultural organisations have always had an artistic strategy that determined the type of art and the specific artists they would present. The new marketing departments were kept carefully separate from the development of the cultural organisation's artistic strategy, so that the cultural product would not be influenced by demands from the marketing department. As a result, it was impossible for them to develop a marketing strategy that included considering the public's needs and desires.

However, it is critical that the marketing department's knowledge of the external environment be considered when defining the organisation's internal artistic strategy. This does not mean that marketing will or should control the cultural organisation or the art form. But it does mean that some compromises to the demands of consumers must be made if the organisation is to survive to present its art.

As the concern over declining attendance continues, professionally managed marketing departments have gained a stronger voice within cultural organisations (Kotler and Scheff, 1997). Also, funding and political pressures from the external environment have made the internal split between artistic and marketing strategy no longer sustainable. The need to increase attendance, while coping with reduced funding, is forcing many cultural organisations to break down the wall between artistic and marketing departments.

This co-operation between the artistic department, which is concerned with the internal mission of the organisation, and the marketing department, which is knowledgeable about the external environment in which the organisation exists, is at the heart of a successful marketing strategy for cultural organisations.

The Mission-Centred Cultural Organisation

Non-profit cultural organisations have a unique role in the marketplace because they provide goods/services that for-profit firms cannot, or will not, provide. Because non-profit organisations provide these goods and services without the incentive of profit, the organisation receives benefits in the form of subsidies and privileges from the civic authorities, either local or federal, which are not available to for-profit firms. There is no incentive for a non-profit organisation to earn excess funds, as they are not allowed to use the funds to enrich the managers of the organisation. This fact, along with the fact that cultural organisations could count on subsidies, resulted in them not even attempting to cover costs with revenue.

Current funding cuts and the resulting pressure to generate revenue is breaking down the strict demarcation between how non-profit and profit firms view profit. Non-profit organisations increasingly have revenue-producing activities that compete with business. For example, a non-profit cultural organisation may have a gift shop or café that competes with local firms by providing similar goods and services. While gift shops and cafés are now common activities, some cultural organisations also have very sophisticated business enterprises including mail-order operations, video production, rental of premises, owning parking garages and even renting/selling their product.

However, there remains an important distinction between these two types of organisations. A popular culture company in the for-profit world may hire an artist but they can, if necessary, change the artist's product to the point where it is unrecognisable to the original creation. The company can even drop the product it was originally producing and produce an entirely new form of popular culture, if that is what the marketplace wants. Because the creator or artist is in the employment of the profit-making company, it can use the product in any way that is necessary to attract customers and make a profit.

But the non-profit cultural organisation cannot change the artist's product to fit the marketplace. The organisation starts with a mission to present the art produced by an individual artist and it must remain true to the artist's vision. But the cultural organisation can remain true to the art form and artist, while at the same time it packages and markets the product in a new manner to the public.

This is the unique challenge faced by cultural organisations when marketing. Fortunately, it is possible to remain mission-driven, while at the same time borrowing marketing strategies from for-profit businesses. In fact, marketing strategies from the fields of broadcasting, publishing/recording, multimedia, sport/leisure and tourism can be very useful. Such companies are closely related to non-profit cultural organisations as they also use creative talent to create products that provide the benefits of both enrichment and entertainment. In fact, such profit and non-profit cultural organisations often compete to provide their product to many of the same customers.

Categorising the Arts

Performing:	*Theatre*
	Dance (Ballet, Modern, Folk, etc.)
	Music (Symphony, Jazz, Popular, etc.)
	Opera
Media:	*Installation Art*
	Film (Narrative, Documentary, Avante garde, etc.)
	Computer/Digital Art
Visual:	*Painting*
	Sculpture
	Crafts (Weaving, Ceramic, Basketry, etc.)
Literary:	*Fiction*
	Poetry

Source: McCarthy, 2001.

ART FORMS, ORGANISATIONS & VENUES TODAY

Trying to define and group art forms is difficult today. The old categories of music, dance, visual art and opera are not the only means of expression that are now considered art. One system is to classify the arts into four main areas of performing, media, visual and literary (McCarthy, Brooks, Lowell and Zakaras, 2001). It is interesting to note the inclusion of media with sub-disciplines of installation art and computer/digital art as of equal ranking in the list. These art forms present unique marketing challenges because it is difficult to define them using the traditional terms of product and venue.

Although difficult to define for the newer art forms, the idea of place or venue is still central to most cultural organisations, with some art forms being more tied to a specific type of venue than others. The visual arts of painting and sculpture have traditionally been very dependent on having a venue for showing their art, usually in the form of a museum or gallery. But today the venue could also be a shopping centre or office complex. And, now with technology, the gallery may even be in cyberspace rather than in a building at all. The relationship between the art form, venue, and organisation needs to be re-examined if the cultural product is to be marketed in new ways.

Relationship Between Art, Venue and Organisation

Art Form	Venue	Organisation
Classical Music	Orchestral Hall	Orchestra
Painting/Sculpture	Museum/Gallery	Foundation
Ballet/Dance	Theatre	Dance Company
Play	Theatre	Theatrical Company
Opera	Opera Hall	Opera Company
Installation Art	?	?
Computer/Digital	?	?

Venues & Funding Pressure

Small theatre, music and dance companies are not as dependent on a specific venue. Because they have always had to be both frugal and customer-conscious to survive, they have performed where they could, to whoever was interested. However large orchestras, ballet companies or operas, because of staging requirements, find they are dependent on having a formal site for presenting their art form. As a result, these organisations must raise additional revenue to pay for this infrastructure. Often, they then become focused on the marketing issues involved in fundraising rather than on marketing to consumers.

This need for securing funding often makes the organisation a hostage to raising money from the government, corporations and patrons. The problem is that all three of these groups often have very different views of the purpose of the organisation. Each has historically supported cultural organisations because they have each had their own vested interest in the survival of the art organisation. Now the objectives each of these three groups has had are changing and the organisations are finding it difficult to cope with the resulting changed expectations.

The government, for one, is no longer willing to continue funding the traditional high arts at the same level and, at the same time, is pressuring these large cultural institutions to be more accessible and answerable to all groups of citizens. Corporate groups, while still willing to support the traditional high arts, are more demanding of the services they receive in exchange. They now frankly state that, in return for support, they want the cultural organisation to provide them with increased visibility, while providing them with opportunities to entertain their clients. Meanwhile, the traditional wealthy patron group is growing older and not being replaced.

Reinventing the Museum

The Royal Ontario Museum (ROM) decided that the only way to keep up with the forces of external change and still maintain its mission was to reinvent itself. The old structure had museum administration as the arbitrator between the departments dealing with exhibits and the curatorial departments. There was no sense of overall strategic objectives and no means to combine the skills and resources that existed in the different departments. But it is exactly this combination that results in the synergy that fuels creativity.

So the ROM implemented a completely different management structure, consisting of a museum-wide steering committee to decide on funding for competing cross-departmental projects. The selection criteria was the extent to which the projects were multidisciplinary, supported by a business case that includes outside partnerships, able to attract a variety of audiences and were supportive of the mission of the museum.

An example of what can be created is the new Discovery Centre. It allows visitors to be involved in the current, ongoing research of the museum. Here visitors can see the actual objects and knowledge being discovered and assessed, rather than only viewing them after they have been safely curated and exhibited.

And now the next step is the creation of 20 new galleries. To keep the community involved in the process, the ROM has opened a new exhibit that is dedicated to the gallery development process.

Source: Sharp, 1998 and Royal Ontario Museum, 2003.

SECTORS OF CULTURAL PRODUCTION

According to a Rand Corporation study, the time when the important distinction was between non-profit organisations creating high culture and for-profit organisations creating popular culture has passed (McCarthy, 2001). The new world will consist of large *versus* small organisations. They see the future of cultural production as consisting of a small number of large:

- For-profit firms producing popular culture products.
- Non-profits that provide high quality arts experiences.

In additional there will be many small:

- For-profit firms that target niche audiences.
- Non-profit arts organisations that provide arts to local and specialised (ethno-cultural) markets.

- Amateur arts organisations that offer people an opportunity to use creative talents for the benefit of friends and neighbours.
- Arts organisations embedded into other institutions, such as universities, that provide arts outside major metropolitan areas.

The Rand report states that the large, well-known non-profit cultural organisations have the endowment and brand name recognition to survive even in a difficult future. For the other cultural organisations, the report sets out four alternatives.

First, they might seek additional funding to grow, bring in star artists or exhibits and become brand names themselves. Second, they might focus on a specialised art for a niche market. Third, they might keep funding down by using local talent and focusing on a local audience. Or, fourth, they might cease to exist.

> ### *"The Great Unspoken Truth About Classical Music"*
>
> *"Classical music is in trouble. Sales of classical music CDs constitute just five per cent of the CD market, concert audiences are shrinking and greying, and younger people aren't taking up the slack ... Buried with that larger problem is another. Classical music is failing to reach the culturally diverse parts of the UK. It is overwhelmingly a white art form, in terms of practitioners (the number of black players in Britain's full-time orchestras could be counted on the fingers of both hands) and, of course, audiences. This has always been the case, but now that cultural diversity has moved to the top of the funding agenda, it's become a serious political embarrassment. There's something disquieting, in 2003, about the sight of all-white orchestra playing to an all-white audience."*
>
> *Source*: Hewitt, 2003.

LIFE CYCLE OF CULTURAL ORGANISATIONS

The product life cycle theory holds that products have a period of introduction, growth, maturity and decline. It may be argued that art as a product is eternal and, therefore, not subject to this theory. However this is not true of art, or of cultural organisations, which also have a predictable life cycle. Museums, dance companies, orchestras and theatres all have histories as organisations. They were introduced as a new, needed organisation to exhibit or present the work of an artist or art form. The organisational life cycle can be described as having seven stages (Bridges, 2003):

Life Cycle of Organisations

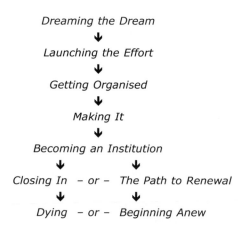

Dreaming the Dream
⬇
Launching the Effort
⬇
Getting Organised
⬇
Making It
⬇
Becoming an Institution
⬇   ⬇
Closing In   – or –   *The Path to Renewal*
⬇   ⬇
Dying   – or –   *Beginning Anew*

Most cultural organisations were formed to provide a cultural product to which the majority of the public did not have access. The founders *dreamed the dream* of providing their art to this public. As a result, the founder's first task was to *launch the effort* by finding funding and developing an audience. If the cultural organisation survived the initial stage, it had to *get organised* with formal departments, including marketing. As the community became aware that the organisation provided a wanted benefit, attendance grew and the organisation *made it* by becoming successful. The cultural organisation would then *become an institution* with a well-known brand name.

However, at this stage, the organisation also faces the risk of losing its audience to a new and younger competitor. If the organisation was very successful in attracting attendance, other existing or new organisations might choose to copy their success by providing the same benefits and targeting similar consumers. At this point in the life cycle, marketing would be difficult as each organisation tried to get their message heard by a limited number of consumers. Or, in the face of increased competition, the organisation may focus inward on its own internal problems and forget its mission to the public.

Therefore, even after a strong history, eventually a period of atrophy or decline can follow, when the attendance slowly starts to decrease due to new competitors or internal organisational problems. Many cultural institutions both large and small find themselves in this position.

The organisation now has a choice. It can *close in* and focus internally on its problems. If it does so, no new ideas of energy will result and it will *die*.

Or its difficulties can force it to a path of *renewal* where it can examine again its dream. Instead of closing in, the organisation needs to revitalise itself by re-examining its mission. This revitalisation can only occur if the cultural organisation takes the opportunity to analyse the cultural product it offers for its current relevance to consumers. This does not mean that the cultural organisation needs to change the art it is presenting. But if the style of presentation, additional services provided or the type of promotions used is no longer appealing to the public, these may need to be changed. Then the cultural organisation is ready to *start anew*.

CHALLENGES FACING CULTURAL ORGANISATIONS

In summary, the marketing challenges cultural organisations face today that require a new marketing strategy include:

- Decrease in consumer time for leisure.
- Expansion of consumer entertainment options.
- Expanded exposure to the world's cultural products.
- Blurring of the distinction between high and popular culture.
- Changing patterns in public funding.
- Organisations at the end of their life cycle.

Some cultural organisations have already been adapting to these challenges by finding new, creative approaches to packaging and marketing their art that have been successful in attracting culture consumers who would not otherwise attend. These cultural organisations understand that the new external environment presents them with new realities that must be faced. These realities include:

- Art can no longer be treated as having a sacred right to public support.
- Cultural marketers can no longer assume that they know what the consumer wants from the cultural experience.
- Consumers living in a multimedia, cross-cultural environment will want more combinations of art forms and new delivery methods.
- Cultural marketers must target packaged events to specific market segments.
- These packaged events must provide multiple benefits to meet consumer needs, while fitting within consumers' time and budget constraints.

There are creative thinkers working in marketing departments at cultural organisations who have developed strategies on how these challenges and realities can be met, while still being true to the artistic vision of the organisation. It is important that others learn of these successes so that cultural organisations can survive to enrich the lives of individuals while serving the community at large.

Business and the Arts

It is not only the arts that gains from collaboration between the art and business worlds. Arts & Business was founded in the UK in 1978 to help the arts to benefit from the professional skills and financial support of the corporate sector. But the organisation also believes that businesses gain from a creative relationship with the arts. In answer to the question of why a business should invest in the arts they respond: "The arts have a unique way of working that can help bring creative thought into your business, and help individuals to enhance their skills and gain fresh inspiration."

Source: Arts & Business, 2004.

There is another important reason to ensure that cultural organisations survive. The world is continually faced with new problems caused by a shrinking globe and an expanding pace of change. The creativity that is the forte of cultural organisations can be used in finding responses to these challenges. In fact cultural organisations can provide an example of innovation in the face of change to other types of organisations.

A Contemporary Look at the Jewish Past in Krakow, Poland

The new Galicia Jewish Museum's main exhibit is "Traces of Memory – A Photographic Exhibition in Tribute to the Jews of Galicia". The museum beautifully and respectfully focuses on a tragic past and yet it is much more. It is not content to just have its viewers intellectually understand its exhibits. It is intent on engaging its visitors so that they emotionally understand what has been lost. The museum then goes one step further by offering activities that in some small measure bring the past again to life. Museum visitors can join in:

- *Concerts showing the influence of Jewish musicians.*

- *Lectures/debates/discussions on historical and theological topics.*

- *Hebrew lessons (these were requested by university aged Poles).*

While its mission is serious, the museum does not consider this to conflict with their mission to make a visit a pleasant experience. The museum also offers a bookstore, gift shop and café.

All of this effort results in a museum that builds a relationship with its visitors so they will want to visit more than once!

Source: Galicia Jewish Museum, 2004.

To survive, cultural organisations must open their doors and invite the world into their institutions, even if the standard of cultural appreciation and knowledge of every consumer is not all the organisation or artist could wish for. Just as churches, temples and mosques welcome those who are sinners, so cultural organisations should also welcome those who are not culturally "pure". Everyone cannot be a saint or artist, but everyone can benefit from contact with them. But the cultural organisation, just like the churches, must do more than open the door: they must invite, welcome and provide for their audience.

This book is meant for those working in the arts or studying arts management who realise that the high quality of their product does not automatically result in a large, appreciative audience. The information it contains can be used by both managers and arts marketers working in a broad range of organisations that deal in all types of cultural products. These managers and marketers may work in nonprofits but they understand that just like their counterparts in profit companies, they have the responsibility of ensuring that there is an audience so that the bills can be paid. What separates them from for-profit companies is their commitment to a mission of sharing their art to enrich the life of the community.

Marketing Plan Worksheet

Having a plan and timeline is important to keep you on track as you start developing a new marketing strategy. Be realistic when assigning responsibilities and deadlines. If you achieve your goal early great! If you fall behind you might become discouraged.

Who is available to assist in the development of a marketing plan?

Task	Person Responsible	Due Date
External Analysis		
Competitor Analysis		
Marketing Audit		
Buyer Motivation		
Segmentation Analysis		
Research Plan		
Product Analysis		
Place Analysis		
Pricing Analysis		

References

Arts & Business (2004) "Press Release: Arts & Business – Gives Business the Chance to SEE for Themselves" online at www.aandb.org.uk.

Björkegren, D. (1996) *The Culture Business*, Routledge.

Bridges, W. (2003) *Managing Transitions: Making the Most of Change*, Persus Publishing.

Cappo, J. (2003) *The Future of Advertising: New Media, New Clients, New Consumers in the Post-Television Age*, McGraw Hill.

DiMaggio, P. (2000) "Social Structure, Institutions, and Cultural Goods: The Case of the United States" in *The Politics of Culture: Policy Perspectives for Individuals, Institutions, and Communities*, The New Press.

Fort Wayne Philharmonic (2004) "Concert Details" online at www.fortwaynephilharmonic.com/fwp/concert_details.

Galicia Jewish Museum (2004) online at www.galiciajewishmuseum.org.

Getty Museum (2004) online at www.getty.org/about.

Heilbrun, J. and Gray, C. (2001) *The Economics of Art and Culture: An American Perspective*, Cambridge University Press.

Hewitt, I. (2003) "The Great Unspoken Truth about Classical Music" in *The Daily Telegraph*, October 18.

Keates, N. (1999) "Why are Museums so Clueless?" in *Arts Reach*, April.

Kotler, P. and Scheff, J. (1997) *Standing Room Only: Strategies for Marketing the Performing Arts*, Harvard Business School Press.

McCarthy, K., Brooks, A., Lowell, J. and Zakaras, L. (2001) *The Performing Arts in a New Era*, The Rand Corporation.

Norris, S. (1997) "Where Commerce Meets Culture" in *Museum Journal*, December.

Putnam, Robert D. (2001) *Bowling Alone: The Collapse and Revival of American Community*, Simon & Schuster Adult Publishing Group.

Royal Ontario Museum (2003) "Views of Our Future: The New Galleries" online at www.rom.on.ca/news/releases/public.

Sharp, L. (1998) "Making Museums More Creative" in *Arts Reach*, October.

Staniszewski, M.A. (1995) *Seeing is Believing: Creating the Culture of Art*, Penguin.

Sweetman, J. (1998) *The Enlightenment and the Age of Revolution 1700–1859*, Longman.

Vandashop (2004) online at www.vandashop.co.uk.

Chapter Two

FROM HIGH ART TO POPULAR CULTURE

One of the basic premises of this book is that changes in the external environment have resulted in a new type of audience member: culture consumer. Culture consumers fundamentally differ from the traditional audience members in how they view and consume culture. Culture consumers are the result of the current generation not being socialised to view high art as inherently more valuable than the popular culture that has been the shaping force of their lives. Also, the opportunity to travel, along with new communications technology, means the current generation have been exposed to cultural traditions from around the world and, therefore, no longer view Western culture as inherently superior to other cultural traditions.

Cultural consumers also differ in that, rather than limiting themselves to participating in only one type of cultural activity, they want to enjoy both high *and* popular culture and both Western *and* foreign cultural experiences. In fact, they have no objection to having them combined in the same cultural event. Before these profound changes can be fully appreciated, it is important to understand how the distinction between high art and popular culture came about in Western society.

HIGH *VERSUS* POPULAR CULTURE

In order to develop marketing strategies that will be successful in attracting culture consumers, it is important to understand the historic distinction between high art and popular culture. The traditional distinction is that high art is produced from the internal vision of the artist, resulting in an artistic product with a unique and personal meaning. When producing high art, the artist has little or no concern for the desires and needs of the consumer who may ultimately purchase the art or view the performance. The art is the product of the artist's inner vision alone, with no consideration given to shaping the art for consumer purchase.

On the other hand, the distinctive feature of popular culture is that the focus is placed on the consumer and the meaning is determined by how they consume the cultural product. Therefore, the desires and needs of the consumer are of paramount importance in the production of popular culture. If consumers change their desires, the producer will give them a new popular culture product.

Of course, such purist positions have always been the extreme. Because of the necessity of making a living, artists who produce high art often care what the future purchasers of their art might want. And artists producing popular culture may have been formally trained in the arts and produce an art product that results from an inner vision.

The historical distinction between high and popular art has been of great importance to cultural organisations. In fact, the mission statements of cultural organisations may have been written with a view toward keeping their art pure from the contamination of the desires of the marketplace. One of the outcomes of the process of developing a marketing plan can be a re-examination of the boundary the organisation has drawn between high art and popular culture, and how much of this distinction is actually important. Without threatening their mission, the cultural organisation can often attract cultural consumers by blending features of popular culture into their marketing strategy. This is especially crucial now that there is less concern among both artists and culture consumers of the boundary between high art and popular culture.

It is interesting to note that the strict boundary between high and popular culture is relatively recent. It was developed in Europe and the US during the 19th century as a reaction to the industrial revolution, the resulting mass production of goods and the rise of the new middle class. The start of a new century is a good time to realise that the distinction between high and popular culture is again blurring.

Arts Marketing is Happening Everywhere!

The Johannesburg Civic Theatre went from selling 20% of their seats to 90% in only three years. How? By positioning the theatre as an entertainment centre rather than an intimidating palace of arts and culture. On its website, the theatre now describes itself as "a thriving, buzzing melting pot of cultures and artistic interests".

Source: Africa News, 2003 and the Johannesburg Civic Theatre, 2004.

DEVELOPMENT OF THE CULT OF HIGH ART

The idea of art produced by a professional artist solely for contemplation, and not use, is a recent phenomenon. The idea of an object as the individual expression of an artist with no utilitarian function became accepted only in the 18th century (Staniszewski, 1995). Prior to this time, art was considered an extension of a society's culture. This culture was expressed through its art, but also through its language, religion, and customs. This art, or better termed in this context as artefacts, included both performance and objects that were the visible production of the society's values and beliefs. The artefacts were produced not as art, even though they may now be considered art, but to meet specific human needs. These needs were pragmatic ones, such as creating pottery dishes for eating, but they also included spiritual needs, such as statues or figures for worship. The creation of both types of objects, those to meet pragmatic and spiritual needs, expressed the culture of the society, not the vision of an individual artist.

It is a modern invention to think of an individual's inner vision as necessary to produce art. In earlier historical times, only technical skills were considered necessary to produce the artefact. The artefact might have been considered beautiful or meaningful by its users, but the first purpose of the artefact was for it to be useful. And technical skill, not vision, was considered necessary to produce the art/object.

This Thing Called Art

"The term 'ART' as we now understand it began to take on its modern meaning in the 18th century: an original creation, produced by an individual gifted with genius. This creation is primarily an object of aesthetic beauty, separate from everyday life. Not solely political propaganda, not a religious nor sacred object, neither magic nor craft, this thing called Art did not exist before the modern era."

Source: Staniszewski, 1995.

During the Renaissance, art was elevated above the level of a mechanical skill. Although the creation of art was still seen on the same level as any of the other traditional areas of knowledge. It was not until the 18th century that the fine arts were separated from the other liberal arts. Then vision and genius were added to technical skill as essential for the production of art. While fine artists might have wished to gain technical skill so as to create their vision, to be considered an artist the vision or genius had to exist first. Since genius was rare, the creations of such artists would have value as a scarce commodity besides their intrinsic value as art.

Those in positions of civil or royal power were always able to purchase the products of artists. With the rise of the market economy, merchants also now had the wealth to purchase art. These merchants may have purchased art because they wished to enjoy the beauty of the object and the satisfaction of sharing in the artist's unique vision. However the value of art did not come only from the object itself, it also resulted from the scarcity of the art object (Budd, 1995). Merchants understood the value of a scarce commodity and also bought art because it could be resold at a profit.

Once the art object could be mass-produced mechanically, it lost its scarcity value and, as a result, was no longer considered high art. If the art object is mass-produced, it can then be purchased by the middle, or even lower, classes. The object will then be frowned upon by many of those who could afford to buy the original art. It is the idea of exclusivity and elitism that results from originality and therefore scarcity, which is sought after by those who can afford it. The copy, no matter how skilfully done, is deemed vulgar. Because it is widely available, popular culture cannot be used as a status symbol in the same way as high art.

For Both Ballet and Crossword Fans!

The New York City Ballet website is not all serious. In fact, if you are in the mood for a crossword puzzle that also tests your knowledge of ballet, go to their website and find crosswords with such clues as:

> *1 Across – a former music director of the NYC Ballet.*
> *or*
> *20 Down – Balanchine ballet set to music by Virgil Tomson.*

Answers are thoughtfully provided.

Source: New York City Ballet, 2004.

Early Cultural Stratification

An example of how art became stratified is the founding in London at the end of the 18th century of the Concert of Antient Music. Its purpose was to raise the standard of music performance and appreciation, particularly among the new professional class. The Society had a rule that only music composed over 20 years previous to performance could be part of the repertoire. The music of Purcell, Corelli, Handel and other English and a few Italian composers was performed. This emphasis on "old" music was to protect the audience from vulgar contemporary music – Italian opera. The founders believed that the public concerts of Italian opera music pandered to the lower classes and degraded music.

In fact the repertoire was considered "classical" because it did not include Italian opera, the popular music of the day. Italian opera performances were what most of the upper middle class and nobility, along with the lower classes of society, attended for entertainment. The orchestral music at these operas was often performed by amateur musicians and entertainment of the audience, not quality of the music, was considered the most important criteria for success. While a member of the upper classes could attend Italian opera for entertainment, it was not considered possible that classical music could be appreciated by those low on the social scale (Shera, 1939).

The founders of the society were not members of the nobility. But they closely identified themselves with the nobility who were seen as the natural patrons of the arts. The founders, who were mostly upper class, sought to present concerts that they considered worthy of a noble audience, while at the same time finding a middle class audience worthy of the music. The goal was to reproduce for the public the private performance of music available to the nobility. These concerts gave members of the upper and middle classes the opportunity to become part of the social world, at least in a limited way, of the nobility. This was the first attempt to promote a public concert series to a particular class of audience (Weber, 1992).

So, by the last quarter of the 18th century, the music world was already splitting into two opposing factions: the modern/popular group that attended Italian opera *versus* the classical/good music group that attended concerts promoted by the Concert of Antient Music. This split along class lines has remained with us.

Shakespeare in the US

Despite early efforts to separate high art from popular culture, the stratification of culture in the production of art for consumers was not always strictly enforced. For example, in the mid-1800s in the United States, art forms such as Shakespearean plays and opera were routinely presented in front of audiences that consisted of people from all social classes and were "simultaneously popular and elite" (Levine, 1988). In these productions, the art was not treated as a sacred text that had to be reverently recreated. Because society had changed since the play had originally been created, those producing the performance felt it perfectly acceptable to alter the script to increase the enjoyment of the audience. It was also considered acceptable for the audience to noisily show their approval – or disapproval – of the performance. Theatre and other art forms were considered part of the general culture that anyone was free to enjoy (or not to enjoy).

It was only in the second half of the 19th century that the self-appointed guardians of culture decided that culture was not for entertainment but only for enlightenment. During this period, the

United States experienced mass immigration and the cultural behaviour of the new immigrants was very unsettling to those who saw themselves as part of the established culture of the United States. As a result, there was a move by those involved in producing cultural events to make this new audience conform to accepted standards of behaviour. This cultural establishment decided that theatres, concert halls and museums were no longer to be seen as places of entertainment. There were now to be institutions with a higher purpose: the improvement of the new masses.

The Birth of the Serious Music Concert in the US

"Thus, by the early decades of this century, the changes that had either begun or gained velocity in the last third of the 19th century were in place: the masterworks of the classic composers were to be performed in their entirety by highly trained musicians on programs free from the contamination of lesser works or lesser genres, free from the interference of audience or performer, free from the distractions of the mundane; audiences were to approach the masters and their works with proper respect and proper seriousness, for aesthetic and spiritual evaluation rather than mere entertainment was the goal."

Source: Levine, 1988.

Victorian England

Meanwhile, in England, the Victorian ideal was to use culture both to improve the working class and to train the new emerging middle class. The Victorian establishment saw culture as a means to produce a sober, hard-working middle class that would accept what the upper, established classes told them was acceptable culture. This new middle class was also told the manner of behaviour that was expected in the theatre, concert hall and museum (Pointon, 1994).

There was never an intention from these custodians of culture to keep the public away. They simply wanted to make sure the public enjoyed the proper culture in the proper manner. And they got to decide what the proper culture was and decreed that the proper manner was to enjoy cultural productions quietly and individually. No longer was raucous expression of approval or disapproval to be allowed. Any behaviour that suggested mass enthusiasm by the crowd was suspect, as it might be followed by uncontrolled behaviour. And the establishment felt that such behaviour might put its status at the top of the hierarchy at risk.

Society is only now moving away from the resulting sacralisation of culture that started in the 18th century and was with us for most of the 20th century. In the 21st century, people are no longer willing to accept being treated as uneducated outcasts who must be taught what culture is best and how it should be enjoyed. The new culture consumers question why they should take their valuable time to learn from others how to enjoy culture that seems, at first exposure at least, to be unenjoyable.

Defining Art in the 19th Century

"The meaning of culture itself was being defined and its parameters laid out in ways that would affect culture profoundly throughout this century. The primary debate was less over who should enter the precincts of the art museum, the symphony hall, the opera house as over what they should experience once they did enter, what the essential purpose of these temples of culture was in the first place."

Source: Levine, 1988.

THE RISE OF POPULAR CULTURE & THE MASS MARKET: THEODOR ADORNO

With the arrival of mass media the effect on society of the ability to mass-produce art was studied with much concern. The ability to record and reproduce music, create copies of art work and film theatrical performances was pronounced to have a negative impact on the public's appreciation of the real art object or performance. (Much the same argument is used today regarding art in virtual reality.) It was feared that exposure to these reproductions would result in individuals no longer seeking meaning in art because their senses would become dulled by constant exposure.

The philosopher Theodor Adorno was greatly concerned that the mass production of music and other cultural products would result in an inevitable homogenisation of art (Adorno, 1998). He believed that such homogenisation would result in a passive consumption of art and, as a result, art would no longer have any deeper meaning. Since he believed the purpose of art was to communicate new ideas, he was concerned that constant repetition of a limited amount of messages would cease to communicate. And as a result, art would lose any meaning. His fears regarding popular culture still echo with some cultural theorists in organisations and academia today.

The belief that high art has a deeper meaning to communicate which is beneficial to society was well established by the mid-20th century. In fact, after the Second World War, governments increased funding to support cultural organisations presenting high art in a belief in its beneficial effect on a population traumatised by war. But during the same time period, there was also an explosion in the commercial creation and consumer demand for popular culture. Because companies that produce the products of popular culture cannot rely on government funding, they must respond to the desires of the consumer. The worldwide popularity of popular culture attests to the fact that they have been very successful in doing so.

The cultural organisation, like Adorno, may believe that high art improves the lives of those who share in its expression. But cultural organisations must accept that the dream of a universal interest in high art has never materialised and that there has always been a limited number of people who wish to experience such cultural events. Cultural organisations must face the fact that, if they are to survive, they can no longer be passive and must now compete actively with popular culture for their audience. This is because the public that desires and consumes popular culture no longer believes that high art is always worthy and that popular culture is always vulgar.

Even if the general public does not wish to support the high art form that the cultural organisation was originally formed to present, the organisation will still want to both preserve and share their art with the public. For this to be possible, they need to have members of the general public attend and come to share in the artistic experience, even if the public may not believe in the art form in the same way as those who manage the organisation.

Therefore, the cultural organisation presenting high art has a unique and challenging task. They must produce and market high art so as to attract an audience of culture consumers raised on popular culture, without compromising the vision of the artist who created the art.

LEVELS OF CULTURE: HERBERT GANS

It is important for those managing cultural organisations to understand why different segments of society patronise different types of cultural events and art forms. Besides Adorno, other theorists have tried to describe why the differences exist. For example, cultural life was defined by Herbert Gans as consisting of four strata: high, middle class, lower middle class and working class cultures (Gans, 1977).

High Culture

In the strata of high culture, the art product is seen as a unique creation of the artist. The art that is created is the external expression of the artist's vision. While it may be difficult, it is still considered the responsibility of the audience to discover and understand the meaning of the vision in order to appreciate the art. It is argued that, when members of the audience can reach this level of understanding, they can share in the genius of the artist. In this view, this is the reason that the art forms of high culture require a prior knowledge of art and artists before they can be enjoyed. In fact, under this theory, art that is widely popular cannot be considered high art, since it is being appreciated by a large audience that would not have this prerequisite knowledge.

This argument explains why the high culture art forms of classical music, ballet and serious theatre receive the most attention from art funders, while they actually attract the smallest audience. This is because the audience, by definition, can only consist of individuals with the high level of education necessary to decipher the meaning. They also must have an interest in doing so, which is often learned only from living with a family of high social class or from pursuing advanced education.

Gans's Levels of Culture

Culture Class	Education Level	Art	Audience
High	High birth/ education	Focus on artist	Responsibility to interpret
Middle class	Professional education	Focus on audience	Desires understandable meaning and enjoyment
Lower middle class	No higher education	Expresses values of society	Easily understandable; unambiguous message
Working class	Limited education	Action oriented; stereotype characters	Relaxation; escapism

Middle Class Culture

Gans ranks middle class culture next in the hierarchy of cultural life. Here, the manner in which art is created and presented switches from focusing on the vision of the artist to the desires of the audience. The audience puts equal importance both on understanding the message the artist wishes to convey and enjoying the art product.

The audience for middle class culture consists of professional members of society. Being in a profession, they have an education that has prepared them to think critically and to enjoy balancing the various, and sometimes contradictory, opinions that art contains. They do not disregard the importance of the artist as the creator of the work, but the artist is mostly important as the producer of the art that the individual either enjoys or does not. The artist becomes the brand name whose work will then be sought out, or avoided, in the future.

Lower Middle Class Culture

Lower middle class is the third strata of cultural life defined by Gans. For this audience, the enjoyability of the content of the art is most important. The audience still wants the art to have a message, but it is not the message of the individual artist that is of interest. The audience desires art with a message that is easily understandable, makes a clear distinction between right and wrong, and expresses the values of conventional society.

Since the members of this audience are usually without a professional education, they lack the power that results from social position, and often feel constrained by the rules of society. They do not have the position or the money to avoid the unpleasantness and conflicts of life. Instead, their lives are often bound by the rules and constraints under which they must live. Ambiguity of meaning, which might be tolerated as a part of middle class culture, would not be appreciated by a lower middle class audience.

Since the lower middle class audience desires art that has an enjoyable content and a clear message that conforms to their own beliefs, artists are now clearly in the role of producing art for the audience rather than for themselves. Therefore, the term popular culture, rather than high art, would traditionally be applied to this type of product.

Indian Art: No Longer Exotic

Where once non-Western art was considered exotic, it is now just one more choice on the cultural buffet. Contemporary Indian artists create works that grow out of both their own culture and out of influences from the West. Their work has sparked an increase in demand for modern art in India, but it has also sparked interest in the West. A group of six Indian artists was on display in New York as part of a major five-nation exhibition, "Contemporary Art in Asia: Traditions/Tensions". The exhibit then moved on to Canada and Asia. Rather than Western and non-Western art, there is now an international contemporary art market.

Source: Rahman, 1997.

Working Class Culture

Working class culture is the fourth strata of cultural life. Here the emphasis is again on clear, understandable, enjoyable content with no ambiguity. At this level, the audience will insist on increased entertainment value through the frequent use of action and stereotyped characters. The audience for this art often has little education and works in jobs that are difficult and repetitious.

Therefore, they wish entertainment that is predictably enjoyable and offers the opportunity for relaxation and escapism. They do not wish to risk their limited leisure time and money on the unknown, nor are they interested in entertainment that challenges the *status quo*.

Herbert Gans's description of the levels of culture is still useful today. But what has changed is that today society is no longer as stratified. With mass education a reality, individuals have the opportunity to move up the social hierarchy. And, because of technology, even working-class jobs now require individuals to have a level of education and sophistication unknown in the past. Both of these facts have actually increased the potential audience for high art. At the same time, those working in high social positions are more likely to attend and enjoy popular culture. As a consequence, it is important for those marketing for cultural organisations to understand that they can no longer assume they know what type of culture is desired by different market segments based on income and education demographics.

Is the Funding Situation Really So Serious?

Ask the following American Orchestras that have recently declared bankruptcy:

- *San Jose Symphony*
- *Florida Philharmonic Orchestra*
- *Colorado Spring Symphony*
- *San Antonio Symphony*
- *Tulsa Philharmonic.*

Or how about these sad facts:

- *Boston Ballet cut number of performances by 19%*
- *San Francisco Opera went from 88 to 65 performances*
- *American Museum of Natural History closed Saturday nights*
- *Brooklyn Museum of Art went from four to one special exhibition*
- *Even the Metropolitan Museum of Art has closed galleries, raised admission, and cut staff.*

Sources: Higgins, 2003; Pogrebin, 2003; Ruvo, 2003.

TASTE IN CULTURE: PIERRE BOURDIEU

It is easy to state that something is in "good taste" or "bad taste" without thinking about what these terms actually mean. Back in the 1970s, Pierre Bourdieu, a French sociologist, performed a ground-breaking analysis of taste (Bourdieu, 1996). His study consisted of interviewing people regarding their preferences in art. To take just one segment of this study as an example, individuals were asked for their preference among three pieces of music: *The Well-Tempered Clavier* by Bach, *Rhapsody in Blue* by Gershwin and *The Blue Danube* by Strauss. Bourdieu used the preferences for these and other related art works to determine class differences in taste, which he labelled legitimate taste, middlebrow taste and popular taste.

He found there was a clear preference for each piece of music among people belonging to certain occupational groups. *The Well-Tempered Clavier* was preferred mostly by those working in education and the arts. *Rhapsody in Blue* was preferred by technicians and junior executives, while *The Blue Danube* was preferred by manual workers, clerical workers and shopkeepers.

Legitimate Taste

Previous studies of this type had concluded that the difference in taste resulted from a difference in educational level and, therefore, that education determines taste. But Bourdieu's theory attempted to explain *why* people have a preference for different types of culture.

He theorised that there are two means by which people can gain access to cultural knowledge, which he called cultural capital. One means is by birth into a high social class, which results in the individual growing up surrounded by what is "correct" aesthetically. The other means is through education, ~e the individual learns what are legitimate works of art and ~t way to enjoy them. Although the necessary knowledge ~ed through either birth or education, those born to a consider education as the second best means. ~e appreciation of art forms is innate to their ~not be learned.

Bourdieu's Tastes in Culture

Taste	Music	Profession	Art
Legitimate taste	*The Well-Tempered Clavier*	High-birth or professionals working in education and arts	Engagement of the intellect
Middle-brow taste	*Rhapsody in Blue*	Technicians and junior executives	Appeals directly to everyday experience
Popular taste	*The Blue Danube*	Manual workers, clerical workers and shop keepers	Pleasure through sensory experience

The enjoyment of legitimate high art then is both a result of, and a criterion for, belonging to the upper class. To reject the art is to reject the class to which you belong. On the other hand, the more one knows about and appreciates the art, the more one's social standing is reaffirmed.

If a privileged birth or education is needed to appreciate art, it then stands to reason that art that anyone can enjoy and is easy to understand cannot be art. And, for those with legitimate taste, to enjoy such non-art means they lack the education to recognise the difference. This view of taste states that the engagement of the intellect tells us what is art. Therefore, art that appeals to the emotions and body is by its very nature suspect.

Middle-brow Taste

However, art that does not have the elements of recognisable form or melody can be difficult to appreciate if the viewer has not been trained by birth or education to understand its appeal. Therefore, the class distinction of legitimate taste is reinforced. It is its very detachment from the everyday experience of life that defines legitimate taste.

In contrast, those with middlebrow taste prefer art that appeals directly to their everyday experience. Those with middlebrow taste are interested in art which can have a personal meaning which is why Bourdieu found these audiences preferred *Rhapsody in Blue*.

Popular Taste

Popular taste appeals to working class audiences who are interested in the concrete and not in the abstract. They want pictures they can understand, dancing that looks like something they could do, and music they can hum. Because they want to receive pleasure through sensory experience, they preferred *The Blue Danube*. Unfortunately their very desires and tastes are looked upon as vulgar by those with legitimate taste.

The Distinction

High art that appeals to legitimate taste is purposefully removed from the immediate sensory pleasure afforded by art that appeals to middlebrow or popular taste. High art appeals to those who are born into a social class with a high-income lifestyle and who, as a result, already have an abundance of sensory pleasure in life. However, for those who are born into a life that demands hard work, it is not surprising that they should not only be uninterested in high art that appeals to legitimate taste and requires an aesthetic knowledge to enjoy, but also be offended by it. They are told that, after a hard day's work, they should now work hard at trying to understand art, which to them, is unattractive and incomprehensible.

Unfortunately, there is a tendency for those who have the prerequisite birth or knowledge to understand high art to look down upon those who do not have it. (This tendency is still prevalent today in the use of the term "dumbing down" when popular culture is discussed.) The upper classes can feel superior because those below them remain dominated by ordinary, everyday desires and interests. However, this tendency is not limited to the upper classes, as every class tries to distinguish themselves from the class below based on their taste in art. While the patron of the high arts looks down on the pleasures of the middlebrow audience, the middlebrow audience also looks down on the pleasures of the working class audience.

"Classical Music Goes Shopping"

What happens when a symphony orchestra plays at the local shopping mall? When the Kensington Symphony Orchestra played at Whiteley's Shopping Centre, the audience stopping to listen to the music had a very different composition from those who would be found in a typical classical music concert hall.

Surprisingly, a large proportion of those listening consisted of young men aged 25 to 40, most of whom were from ethnic minorities. What was particularly interesting about the men was the intensity with which they watched the musicians perform. They would get as close as possible, often standing right next to the musicians and they stayed to listen to all styles of music from Brahms to "movie" music.

The Kensington Symphony Orchestra performed for free in the shopping centre to solicit money for a good cause, while at the same time providing a pleasurable addition to the shoppers' day. Unfortunately, bringing classical music to the community is often looked upon by orchestras as a means to edify and educate, rather than simply providing an enjoyable experience for the listeners.

Source: Kolb, 1998.

CULTURAL HIERARCHY TODAY

Despite Adorno's fears, people still find meaning in art. What is different is that the easy availability of all types of culture has resulted in a breakdown in the distinction between high culture and popular culture described by Gans and Bourdieu. Today, the same consumers may enjoy both without concern for labels.

The public no longer looks to the cultural organisation to provide an internal meaning for the art, but to provide the raw material with which individuals can create their own meaning. Individuals in our modern society, particularly the young, are very skilled at deciding what is important to their lives. They no longer look to a single social class, religion, nationality or ethnic group to provide an infrastructure of meaning. People now feel free to create their own meaning and associate with whom they please (Fornas, Lindberg and Sernhede, 1995).

Cultural Buffet

An additional factor affecting cultural organisations is that, through technology and travel, people now have access to cultural products from societies from around the globe. Not only has the old high culture *versus* popular culture boundary been breached, individuals no longer feel tied to Western culture and feel free to pick and choose from many cultural viewpoints and styles. Rather than fit into a hierarchy, they create cultural life by choosing from a range of options both from the different cultural strata and from other cultures worldwide.

Cultural organisations still play a vital role by providing a place where the public can discover cultural meaning. Of course, cultural organisations have always provided this opportunity. The difference is that they are no longer the only arbiters of meaning, as they have been in the past.

Today's culture consumers still desire art, but will no longer accept the authority of the cultural organisation. However, the organisation can still play a critical role in cultural life. They can do so by providing a place for people to associate with others to create their own cultural life in a way that creates or reinforces community.

Cultural life today should be seen as a buffet, rather than a hierarchy. At one end is art that is entirely focused on the producer and, at the other end, art that is entirely focused on the consumer. The range is broad and individuals will choose their cultural activities from anywhere on the buffet to create their own unique cultural life.

Creativity + Technology = New Artists

The availability of computer technology to aid in the creation of artwork has opened the door to many who considered themselves creative but who have previously not gotten involved in traditional art forms. Perhaps this is because technology is now in all offices and most homes, while canvas and paint are not.

Lovebytes in Sheffield (UK) provides multimedia production facilities at subsidised rates for anyone who wants to create. The Lovebytes media lab encourages newcomers to the media by offering both informal assistance and formal training. They also sponsor the Lovebytes Digital Arts Festival where new and established artists can show their work.

Source: Lovebytes, 2004.

TECHNOLOGY & CULTURAL CONSUMER

Technology, specifically information technology, has changed the way in which we view the world. Therefore, it is not surprising that it has also changed the way that people view, react to, and create art. At first, it was feared that using technology to reproduce art would deaden its appreciation (Chanan, 1994). However, it has been found that the opposite is true. Computer technology allows those who would never have been considered artists to be creative. Software programmes allow the non-artist to both compose music and create visual art. And the Internet also gives these new artists a way to display their art to an audience.

Technology has allowed the culture consumer to participate directly in many aspects of daily life in a manner that was previously unthinkable. Technology allows people to purchase everything from automobiles to groceries on their computer, so it is not surprising that they would also purchase tickets to cultural events. This online purchasing means that the "middle person" who previously was relied upon to give advice on what is "good" is now gone. They have been replaced by searching the Internet, which gives the consumer control over the flow of information (Postma, 1999).

Just as the culture consumer is no longer content to rely on authority figures for knowledge, they are also not content to be a passive believer in the superiority of any one form of art. Because they have access to a massive amount of information and art from around the world, they are no longer willing to concede that someone is an artist, just because the art establishment has deemed them to be so (Burnett, 1996).

This is another reason why culture consumers are not willing to be passive consumers of culture but insist in being involved in the decision about what is art, how it is presented and how it should be consumed. The philosopher Jacques Attali called this the composition stage, when everyone would be able to make their own music in a free and decentralised society (Attali, 1996). In the current stage of technological development, everyone can be an artist.

External Analysis Worksheet

The first steps in the marketing process are to state your organisation's mission and to examine the effect of external societal changes.

Our organisation's mission (or reason we exist) is:

External Factor	Recent Change	Effect on Organisation
Our Competition (Other art organisations? Popular culture venues? Technology?)		
Social Changes (Interest in new art forms? Changes in life styles? Time pressure?)		
Demographic Changes (Ethnic markets? Ageing Audience? Young culture consumers?)		
Economic Issues (Funding cuts? Rising unemployment? Decrease in sponsors?)		

Below list the greatest social challenge that is affecting your organisation and how marketing can help address the problem.

Greatest Challenge	Needed Action

References

Adorno, T. (1998) *Aesthetic Theory*, University of Minnesota Press.

Africa News (2003) "South Africa: Artists Need to Develop Brands", May 30.

Attali, J. (1996) *Noise: The Political Economy of Music*, University of Minnesota Press.

Bourdieu, P. (1996) *Distinction: A Social Critique of the Judgement of Taste*, Routledge.

Budd, M. (1995) *Values of Art: Pictures, Poetry and Music*, Penguin.

Burnett, R. (1996) *The Global Jukebox: The International Music Industry*, Routledge.

Chanan, M. (1994) *Musica Practica: The Social Practice of Western Music from Gregorian Chant to Postmodern*, Verso.

Fornas, J., Lindberg, U. and Sernhede, O. (1995) *In Garageland: Rock, Youth and Modernity*, Routledge.

Gans, H. (1977) *Popular Culture and High Culture: An Analysis and Evaluation of Taste*, Basic Books.

Higgins, M. (2003) "When the Show Doesn't Go On: Strapped Arts Groups Scale Back, Cancel Productions: Tap Dancers Replaces Swan Lake" in *The Wall Street Journal*, August 27.

Johannesburg Civic Theatre (2004) online at www.showbusiness.co.za.

Kolb, B. (1998) "Classical Music Goes Shopping" in *Arts Reach*, November.

Levine, L. (1988) *Highbrow Lowbrow: The Emergence of Cultural Hierarchy in America*, Harvard University Press.

Lovebytes (2004) online at: http://www.lovebytes.org.uk.

New York City Ballet (2004) online at www.nycballet.com/programs.

Pogrebin, R. (2003) "City's Art Budget Being Cut in Money Pinch" in *The New York Times*, February 11.

Pointon, M. (1994) *Art Apart: Art Institutions and Ideology Across England and North America*, Manchester University Press.

Postma, P. (1999) *The New Marketing Era: Marketing to the Imagination in a Technology Driven World*, McGraw Hill.

Rahman, M. (1997) "The Arts/Art: A Rich Canvas Fusing Western Styles with Local Passions, India's Flamboyant School of Contemporary Artists is Starting to Gain Serious Attention Both at Home and Overseas" in *Time, International*, February.

Ruvo, Kira (2003) "Arts Reach Briefs" in ArtsReach, May.

Shera, F.H. (1939) *The Amateur in Music*, Oxford University Press.

Staniszewski, M.A. (1995) *Believing is Seeing: Creating the Culture of Art*, Penguin.

Weber, W. (1992) *The Rise of Musical Classics in Eighteenth Century England: A Study in Canon Ritual and Ideology*, Oxford University Press.

Chapter Three

THE NEW CULTURE CONSUMER

The previous chapter described theories on why individuals are attracted to different types of culture. These theories focused on the individual's social class, education and income level as factors that predicted an interest in art. Cultural organisations still describe their audiences using these demographic terms.

However, there is another means of describing the composition of an audience other than demographic characteristics. Rather than grouping the audience by differences in demographics, the audience might be better understood if described by their different level of involvement with the art form.

Abercrombie and Longhurst (1998) used this approach to analyse the members of media audiences. They were not grouped by demographics but by their degree of involvement with the media they choose to watch. The groups that result from this type of analysis can be described as belonging to communities that fall along a continuum from consumer to petty producer. The audience continuum and their relationship to the media and each other is shown below:

Model of Media Use

Consumer: Light and generalised media use.

Fan: Use focused on specific stars and programmes.

Cultist: Heavy, specialised use with associated social activities.

Enthusiast: Serious interest in entire media form with structured activities.

Petty Producer: Amateur producer of media form.

In their model analysing audiences of electronic media, Abercrombie and Longhurst describe *consumers* of media as having a generalised pattern of light media use with unsystematic taste. Consumers do not focus on enjoying only one type of media form or content, but feel free to choose from whatever is available. The consumer's choice of a particular programme to enjoy is based on factors such as convenience and cost. Although they care about the programme content, it is not the only deciding factor in their choice. They may enjoy media with family and friends, but their involvement with the media does not extend to the point where they join in activities with others based on their mutual interest.

Fans of media have become attached to particular stars or programmes and have more frequent and focused media use. When choosing a programme to watch, they will base their choice on specific programme content that they have enjoyed in the past. They are willing to tolerate some additional cost and inconvenience in order to enjoy their choice of media programme. However, they continue to enjoy their choice of media as individuals and, like consumers, do not associate with others with similar interests.

Cultists have become highly specialised in their selection of stars and programmes and have heavy media use. They will make a special effort in terms of cost and convenience to enjoy specific media programmes. They will also take the time to learn about their favourite star's personal life and career. Cultists are distinguished from fans by their participation in activities associated with their choice of media. For example, they will read publications about their interest. They are also distinguished from both consumers and fans by their desire to form a community by joining with other cultists in activities focused on their joint media interests. These are the people who will travel to be a member of the studio audience to see their favourite programme being filmed. They also are likely to travel to visit historical sites associated with the programmes they watch.

When an individual is at the *enthusiast* level of involvement, there is a general appreciation of the media as an art form, without any attachment to particular stars or programmes. Enthusiasts become highly knowledgeable about the media and its creators. For example, film enthusiasts will take classes on the history of cinema.

They also wish to share their enjoyment with others. What distinguishes enthusiasts from cultists is the tight organisational structure of the communities they form. Their involvement with other enthusiasts in activities surrounding their media interest is central to their lives and their value systems. For enthusiasts, their appreciation of the media and involvement in activities with others form an important part of their self-identity. Their social life will be constructed around these activities.

At the extreme of the continuum, *petty producers* become so involved that they start to produce amateur versions of the media. Having their social life revolve around their interest is no longer sufficient. If possible, they will try to find employment that will allow them to be involved daily with others who share their media interests.

Oh, To Be Young Again!

Why? Because you have to be between the ages of 21 and 35 to join New York City Opera's "Big Deal". What is it? A membership in the opera that allows you to purchase tickets for orchestra seats at low cost.
- *Diva Membership is $45 and then you can buy one ticket to every opera for $33 each.*
- *Duet Membership costs $60 but you can then get two tickets for each opera for you and an "opera-loving pal".*

Why else should you join? You get invited to the "Big Party" to kick off the opera season where you can meet fellow opera-goers your own age, which might lead to a Big Romance!

Source: New York City Opera, 2004.

An Example: Football Fans

Although Abercrombie and Longhurst use the model to describe media use, this same model can be used to describe the behaviour of other types of audiences. For example, it helps to understand the model by examining how individuals relate to the game of football. If an individual is only a consumer of football, they may choose to attend an occasional game simply because it is something to do on a Sunday afternoon. They will not be particular about which team is playing, but will base their attendance decision on other factors such as convenient location, price of tickets and amenities offered at the stadium.

In contrast, football fans will follow a particular team and enjoy attending as many of their games as possible. They will be sure to attend the "big game", even if it is in another city and it is raining. If they cannot attend, they make a point of reading the sports pages on Monday to see how their team played.

The cultist will take the next step in involvement by becoming highly knowledgeable of the rules of the game and will know the names and rankings of all the players. They will also associate with other cultists at pre-game events because they enjoy socialising with others who share the same interest in football. If they cannot travel to the game, rather than watch alone at home, they will go to the pub to watch the game with others.

Enthusiasts extend their knowledge of football even further. Their interest extends beyond the career of an individual player or the record of a specific team to the game of football itself. They will become familiar with league business and feel themselves as informed as those involved in running the league. Not only will they attend the game in a group while all dressed in team colours, but also a pre- and post-game party at the local pub. They will travel to other cities, often with the same group of fellow enthusiasts to watch games on a regular basis.

If they reach the level of involvement of a petty producer, they will use their knowledge to coach a youth league. They will then be able to meet and join in league activities with other coaches. If they are rich enough, they will become petty producers by either buying or forming their own team.

Using Action Verbs!

One of the first things you learn when producing promotional materials is to use action verbs to catch the public's attention. The Baltic Contemporary Art Centre in Gateshead has taken that lesson to heart. Rather then the usual visiting of subjects on the first page of their website you will find the following verbs:

- *Begin, View, Live, Visit, Explore, Participate, Remember, Consume, Read, Support.*

Source: Balticmill, 2004.

MODEL FOR CULTURAL EVENT ATTENDANCE

This model based on levels of interest and involvement is also useful to describe different types of cultural event attenders. The extent to which an individual feels associated with the art form and each other can help us to understand the motivation for attending. The cultural organisation can then produce a cultural event and create a marketing strategy that meets these needs. This need might be for a casual evening out or for an evening that is part of a deeper relationship.

For example, culture consumers may be visiting a museum or taking in a matinee at the theatre only as something to do on a rainy day. Fans of culture would always patronise a certain cultural organisation, such as the Victoria & Albert Museum, or special performances, such as musical plays by Andrew Lloyd Webber. Culture cultists can be described as those who have taken the time to learn everything about the artists in a specific art form such as ballet. Enthusiasts of culture take the next step in involvement and know everything about the art form in general and make participating in cultural activities an important part of their life by joining with others in the "Friends" organisation or by going on study tours. People who reach the level of petty producers then produce or collect art themselves. Of course, cultural organisations would like all audience members to be at least fans, if not cultists or enthusiasts. However, due to generational changes in how people view and use culture, the truth is that most audience members are culture consumers.

The aim of the management of cultural organisations has been to turn the consumers of culture into the enthusiasts of culture. It has long been thought by cultural organisations that the means of doing this was through education programmes. They believe that, if only those who are currently mere consumers of culture would receive enough education, they would then understand the art form, feel a deeper appreciation and association, and become enthusiasts.

"Beethoven's Never Been a Problem. It's the Way Beethoven is Presented that's the Problem"

So says John Axelrod, Artistic Director of Orchestra X. Axelrod wanted to conduct an orchestra that played classical music but with "no symphony halls, no overpriced tickets, no suits and ties, and no formality". But to do so he realised he would need to start his own orchestra. Axelrod's research told him that young people are familiar with classical music through exposure in popular culture. He also found that they had no objection to the music, only to attending a concert.

Orchestra X overcomes this hurdle by taking the music to their targeted audience in cafés, coffee-houses and arena theatres, and at these venues the music is presented along with anything from belly dancers to puppets. No silent respectful audience is expected or desired and the audience is allowed to dance, clap and sing along, just as they would while enjoying popular culture.

Do the musicians object to this type of audience? No, since the average age of the musicians is 25 and they are part of the same MTV generation as their audience.

Axelrod understands that the average middle-aged concert attender would not enjoy his concerts but he believes that there are already enough traditional concerts for these enthusiasts to attend. Orchestra X can be different because it has its own organisation and board and does not risk alienating an existing conservative audience.

But do young people respond? Definitely, the concerts sell out and they can't keep up with the calls for tickets. But, if they can't get a ticket, they can always listen to the concert live on the Internet at the orchestra's website, www.orchestrax.org.

Source: Barbieri, 1998 and Bambarger, 2004.

The "Education" of the Culture Consumer

To use visitors to art museums as an example, through educational outreach programmes the museum management hopes that they can move the culture consumer along the continuum from consumer to enthusiast. The museum management understands that the cultural consumer would have only a generalised interest in art and would visit the museum only occasionally as an enjoyable experience perhaps to fill a rainy afternoon. Nevertheless through educational information provided by the museum, it is hoped they would learn to enjoy the art of specific artists. The cultural organisation believes they would then become fans and, therefore, visit the museum more frequently to see the artists' work. Although they would visit museums to see specific artists or schools of art, fans would still have little interest in joining with others in activities focused on art appreciation.

After the fans had gained additional knowledge and expertise on their favourite artists, they would become cultists. Through educational programmes provided by the museum, they would become involved in highly specialised areas of art, such as the pre-Raphaelite brotherhood. These new cultists would continue to increase their involvement by reading specialised books and magazines on the subject that they purchased in the museum gift shop.

Feeling a need for even closer association, cultists would then become enthusiasts, who would wish to be associated more closely with others who share their interest by becoming members or "Friends" of the museum. In addition they would plan their social life around museum events. For them, their association with the museum would become an important part of their identity. They would even go on tours marketed by the museum along with other enthusiasts.

At the extreme of involvement, they would become petty producers and be amateur artists or collectors. They would feel they knew how to manage the museum as well, if not better, than the museum management.

Stages of Audience Involvement with Art Exhibits

Type	Involvement
Culture Consumer	Any museum on a Sunday afternoon
Culture Fan	Attends Monet exhibits
Culture Cultist	Joins local museum association and attends educational events on Monet
Culture Enthusiast	Studies Impressionism art movement; travels to other museums for exhibits, joins "Friends"
Culture Petty Producer	Collects paintings or prints

Culture Consumerism as a Permanent State

However, of course, the transition from consumer to enthusiast is not easy to accomplish. People have many choices on how to spend their limited leisure time, and may not be willing to spend this time learning more about culture. They may not be interested in attaining a higher level of appreciation of culture and may be happy to remain culture consumers. They have no desire to attend educational events designed to deepen their emotional involvement with the art form. Because of this, those working in cultural organisations, who are already enthusiasts if not petty producers, view culture consumers as ignorant. But rather than ignorant, they can also be seen as making an informed choice. They are not willing to spend the required time and energy on learning a deeper appreciation of an art form.

Cultural organisations must accept the fact that, for most people, their level of interest will remain at the consumer level. These consumers desire culture as an occasional activity and this preference is not easily changed. The problem is that most of the people who produce art and manage cultural organisations are at least enthusiasts. Art forms a central part of their identity and it is difficult for them to conceive that culture consumers could be exposed to the art and still wish to remain at the consumer level.

It would be more useful for the cultural organisation, rather than assume that the consumption choices made by the public are faulty, to provide the level of engagement that each segment of the public desires. This will mean a major shift in emphasis for many cultural organisations. They will need to learn to accept culture consumers as they are, rather than as people in need of improvement, and provide cultural events that cater to the different levels of involvement for the different groups.

This means that the cultural organisation will need to meet the needs of two distinct groups. The cultural enthusiasts, who attend regularly, volunteer and donate funds, will need events that allow them to become more involved. The culture consumers will need events that allow them to be entertained. It is necessary to focus on both groups because the cultural enthusiast group is ageing and not being replaced.

From Prole to Culture Vulture

When a Parliamentary Commission held hearings on the fate of the troubled Royal Opera House, Sir Colin Southgate, the Covent Garden chairman, worried aloud that the effort to reach out to new audiences would result in opera attenders wearing "shorts and smelly trainers". On the other side of the argument, Gerry Robinson, who was at that time the new head of the Arts Council, blamed the opera administration for the dominance of "white middle-class audiences". The Independent on Sunday *came down on the side of the Arts Council:*

> *"A pantomime is underway between the defenders of privilege – who want their pleasures subsidised because, well, just because – and those who suggest that the way to widen access to refined pleasures is to make them less refined. It is a hoary old chestnut of the trainer-loathing classes that 'ordinary' people are genetically programmed not to want to enjoy the arts, or that if they do they will find their way there in the end. They all know someone who was born in a hovel, saved up their shilling for his first seat in the gods and miraculously evolved from prole to culture vulture. Of course, they don't expect anything like the same Sisyphean exertions from their own social peers who are introduced to high culture, quite effortlessly, as part of a fulfilled and varied life."*

Source: McElvoy, 1998.

THE AGEING AUDIENCE

Every five years, the US National Endowment for the Arts (NEA) conducts a statistically valid Survey of Public Participation in the Arts (SPPA). The survey asks correspondents about their participation in a variety of art forms including classical music, opera, ballet, plays and art museums.

Since this data is collected every five years, it is useful in tracking changes in attendance demographics, such as the age of audience members (Nichols, 2003). A comparison of all survey participants from 1992 to 2002 shows that the average age increased by three years, which is in line with the overall ageing of the American population. But the average age of participants who attend the arts increased even more than the population as a whole. The jazz audience, although the youngest, also is the audience that has aged the most, with an increase of six years in average age in the period from 1992 to 2002. The average age of those visiting art museums increased by five years, while the audience for classical music and ballet increased by four years. Opera's audience alone aged with the national average. Of all the art forms, only the audiences for musicals and plays aged less than the overall population, but by only one year.

Median Age of Arts Attenders, 1992 and 2002

Category	1992 Medium Age	2002 Medium Age	% Change
All Participants	42	45	+3
Jazz	37	43	+6
Classical Music	45	49	+4
Opera	45	48	+3
Musicals	43	45	+2
Plays	44	46	+2
Ballet	40	44	+4
Art Museums	40	45	+5

Another method of studying this data on ageing of the audience is to examine the data on the percentage of the audience under 35 in relation to the audience as a whole. This reveals the problem as being caused by the decline in young attenders. Ballet has the sharpest decline in young attenders, with a 35.4% change from 1992 to 2002. Jazz has seen a 28.3% decline and both classical music and art museums 21.9%. Opera has the smallest decline, with only a 14.9% drop.

Percentage of Audience Aged 18–34, 1992 and 2002

Age 18–34	% in 1992	% in 2002	% Change
Jazz	42.8	30.7	−28.3%
Classical Music	29.2	22.8	−21.9%
Opera	29.6	25.2	−14.9%
Musicals	32.6	27.4	−16.0%
Plays	33.3	27.6	−17.1%
Ballet	38.3	25.1	−35.4%
Art Museums	39.2	30.6	−21.9%

ATTENDANCE BY YEAR OF BIRTH

The well-known fact that the arts audience as a whole is older than the general population is often used to support the argument that today's young cultural consumer will attend when they get older and become a cultural enthusiast. A National Endowment for the Arts study took a broader view of this issue by using the data from previous arts attendance studies to track whether the changes in attendance were caused by when people were born rather than just their current age. The question that the NEA wanted answered was whether social influences while young affects future attendance.

To answer this question, the data from survey participants over 15 years of age was grouped by birth year and then analysed for attendance patterns. The information supplied by this study is important because of its analysis of how the age groups' attendance patterns varied by birth year for the different art forms.

To perform the analysis, the report divided the population into cohorts based on year of birth, among which were:

- Depression – born between 1926 and 1935.
- Second World War – born between 1936 and 1945.
- Early Boomers – born between 1946 and 1955.
- Late Boomers – born between 1956 and 1965.
- Baby Busters – born between 1966 and 1976.

Each birth-year cohort would have been affected by different social influences as they matured. Social influences result from the prevailing societal conditions, and change over time. For example, the social influences affecting the young today are very different from the social influences that affected the young in the 1960s, and most certainly the 1940s. People growing up in these earlier periods had unique experiences that greatly affected the formation of their values, including their view of culture and arts attendance. These values would stay with them and not change unless affected by another strong contrary socialising influence.

What is Art and Who Decides if it is "Good?"

This has always been a tough question. With the new technologies making the process of creating art available to many, it is a question that is becoming even more difficult to answer. Perhaps there needs to be two separate definitions of quality: one for the artist and his or her fellow artists and one for the public who views the art. Artist Amy Bruckman explains:

> *"While I see the benefit of the creative process to the artist as primary, one can still speak of a secondary benefit of the product to other members of the community – and that is a rough metric for 'quality'. A work that entertains, inspires, enlightens, delights, or disgusts (provokes some significant reaction) in a broad audience can be seen as having a different 'quality' than one appreciated only by its creator. A work exists only in relationship to an audience. It's not meaningful to call something 'better' without saying better for who, when and where, and according to whose judgement. . . . The word artist is broad enough to refer to both the professional and the growing number of amateur artistic communities. To blur the distinction between them is also to blur the distinction between high and popular culture, a phenomenon that has progressed throughout this century. The network is accelerating this blurring, towards a greater pluralism of creative expression."*

Source: Bruckman, 1999.

Generational Shift in Attendance

The NEA study found a generational shift in the attendance rates for the art forms of classical music, opera, ballet, plays and arts museums. However, the change in rates was not uniform but differed among the art forms.

When the study examined generational attendance patterns in classical music, it was found that the highest proportion of attenders were those born during the years of the Second World War, 1936–1945. The lowest level of attenders were those born between 1966 and 1976, the most recent cohort. However it is important to note that the older cohorts had also attended when they were young.

When analysing opera attendance, the report found a similar picture with most attenders from the earlier birth-year cohorts and then a dramatic decline in attendance by those born later. One would conclude that opera is in almost as bad a state as classical music. But the most recent data shows that opera has been able to slow this decline.

Ballet shows a slightly different pattern. The audience for ballet has a higher proportion of members of the Early and Late Boomers than for classical music or opera. Unfortunately, attendance among the Baby Busters shows a further decline.

Attendance at non-musical theatrical performances was also examined. Plays have the highest attendance rate of any of the other art forms contained in the study. While there was a noticeable drop-off in attendance for cohorts born after 1945, attendance still is high enough among the younger groups so that there is no serious concern for the art form as a whole. On the other hand the world of theatre is very diverse and, despite this overall picture, many theatre companies struggle to find any audience at all.

An entirely different picture is found when attendance at art museums is examined. For this art form, there is the exact opposite attendance pattern. The youngest cohort, the Baby Busters, has the strongest attendance rate. The second strongest group is the Late Boomers. Interest in art museums has not been affected by a negative generational values shift. Less attendance by the current younger members of society seems to be part of a natural lifecycle pattern of attendance.

This data demonstrates that cultural organisations cannot assume that the youngest cohort will start to attend just because they age. As described previously, their life experiences have been very different from the older cohorts. For example, the manner of presenting art may seem rigid and authoritarian and not appeal to them. On the positive side, museums have become an activity popular with younger birth year cohorts and it can be predicted that they will continue this activity as they age. Cultural organisations therefore must find a way to present their art in a manner that appeals to less deferential, risk- and excitement-seeking Baby Busters.

Are Subscribers Becoming Extinct?

Subscription sales have been a boon to arts organisations in the past. It takes less time to sell a series of six concerts than six single tickets. However a study of concert attenders shows a generational shift in buying habits. Only 15% of consumers in the 18–34 age range are highly inclined to subscribe while 56% of those aged 75 or older.

In fact, the study of 15 orchestras found that half of subscribers are 65 or older!

Source: Brown, 2003.

Changing Attendance Predictors

From previous research, it has been assumed that age, educational level and income are the most important criteria in predicting attendance. If attendance is primarily an activity of the middle-aged and older, then low attendance by younger individuals is not a problem. All that needs to be done is to wait for them to age! And cultural organisations located in geographic areas that have a higher proportion of young people in the population could anticipate an even larger increase in attendance. Unfortunately the NEA study on birth year cohorts shows that attendance patterns are set while young.

If educational level is the key criteria, this is also good news for cultural organisations. With increased access to higher education becoming the norm, there should be an automatic increase in attendance. If most current attenders have university education, then an increase in society of university graduates should automatically expand attendance. However, again, the facts do not prove the case.

If income is the determining factor, there is little the cultural organisations can do to increase the wealth of society. But, if they assume that wealthy people attend because they have been exposed to culture, the cultural organisation can try to ensure that everyone has the same advantage through outreach programmes to the schools. While well intentioned, such efforts may not be producing the desired results. If they assume that wealthy people attend because they can afford to do so, then the answer is to subsidise tickets for other lower income groups. Again, this has been tried but with limited success.

The decline of attendance among the young is of great concern. These younger birth cohorts have had more access to university education leading to better employment opportunities. However, despite this they mostly have the lowest level of attendance.

What is often forgotten is that a correlation between attendance and such factors as age, education and income does not imply causation. The fact that two or more factors may exist in the target population at the same time does not mean that one causes the other. There must be a reason younger people are not currently attending, and will probably not attend when older.

Education or Socio-economic Status: Which Influences Arts Attendance?

Does educational outreach to schools affect later attendance at the arts? All research seems to show it does, including a research report produced by the US National Endowment for the Arts using 1992 census data. Not only does art education positively affect attendance; the relationship was four times stronger than any of the other predictors. So it would seem more arts education results in more attendance.

However . . .

The NEA kept analysing and they found that actually the predictor for who would receive arts education was socio-economic status. The higher one's income and social status, the more arts education they were likely to receive. And, of course, the more general education one received. It is difficult to untangle the various factors that predict arts attendance, but believing that simply adding arts to the educational curriculum will solve the arts attendance problem of the future is simplistic. For, as the report found, arts education had a more powerful impact on arts attendance when it was received by individuals along with a high education level. But art education alone, without the larger socialisation that advanced education provides, had less impact on future attendance.

Surprisingly, individuals who received both high levels of education and arts education were much less likely to create art. Individuals who received arts education, but a low level of general education, were much more likely to be involved in the creation of art. Perhaps they are creating rather than attending.

Source: NEA Report #36.

VALUE SHIFT

The answer may be in changing social values. Values are moral principles that affect how people live their lives and the choices they make and are not easily changed. They are formed while young by both exposure to the values of family and society and by direct experiences. Values are deep-seated beliefs about how one should live and what is important in life. Values include beliefs about the significance of status, the authority of individuals, the importance of knowledge versus experience, and the relationship between people and culture.

Opera with Meaning for a New Generation

How do you reach out to young people when they come from a cultural group very different from the majority audience and performers? The Lyric Opera of Kansas City in the US developed a programme "Opera for Teens" with the aim of introducing teens to a new art form and also integrating the opera into the teen's learning of history, social studies, humanities and language arts.

The two operas chosen for the programme were Never Lost a Passenger: Harriet Tubman and the Underground Railway, *based on the life of the former slave, and* Joshua's Boots, *which recognises the contributions of African-American cowboys and soldiers. These operas have an immediate meaning to Afro-American students. They still have many years ahead when they can listen to operas set in 18th-century Italy – if they ever want to.*

Source: Fanciullo, 1998/99.

The values of individuals growing up during the 1930s and 1940s would have been shaped by years of depression and war. At that time, society experienced a need for authority so that the crisis years could be survived. Such basic needs as food, shelter and security could not have been taken for granted. The resulting need for security and authority is a deep-seated value that has lasted throughout life.

But the succeeding generation had a very different experience and, as a result, very different values. Those growing up in the 1960s were socialised at a time when individual freedom from authority was emphasised. They have kept the value of social liberalism, even though they have now entered a phase in their life span where, as parents and workers, they may outwardly resemble their parents.

The young adults of the current generation are even more individualistic. They are not concerned with security but instead they seek risk, which makes them very different from preceding generations. The concern for safety and social liberalism that were important to previous generations is taken for granted by the current generation, who now desire excitement.

How to Build Bridges to Ethnic Groups

Increasing interest in ethnic communities in orchestra performances cannot be a one-off event. Such programming will be seen as condescending to the community involved. Instead of having only one concert and then expecting the ethnic community member to "convert" to the orchestra's regular programming, it is better to build bridges by working collaboratively. An example is the concerts presented each year in the US honouring the birthday of the Rev. Martin Luther King, Jr. These concerts, which often focus on music composed by African-Americans, are reaching more new concert attenders each year. But, rather than viewing the concerts as outreach, the orchestras involved treat the concerts as a duty and honour – and the African-American community responds. If outreach even hints at a lack of respect for the choices and values of the target community or group, it is justly doomed to failure.

Source: Truskot, April 1999.

Value Shift among Young Londoners

An example of this generational shift in values is shown in a research report that analysed how the values of Londoners have changed over the generations (Jupp and Lawson, 1997). The report found that Londoners under the age of 45 are less interested in appearance and more interested in experience than the previous generation. They care less about what others think of them and more about how they are enjoying life. Because they have travelled more widely (this is especially true of the under-25 age group), they are much more interested in exploring other cultures and are more accepting of the cultures of others. They distrust traditional institutions that an older generation would have looked to for values and standards. This distrust includes cultural institutions and their products.

The young Londoners studied had grown up in a time free of serious material need. They are not concerned with finding external sustenance and instead are concerned with self-development.

If Adults Won't Come, Why Should Children?

Too many cultural organisations focus on recruiting children simply to replace the adults who are no longer coming. But if the children perceive the event as boring, it can be worse than doing no outreach at all. As Richard Eyre said while Director of the National Theatre in London: "Dull theatre will put off both adults and children, but adults might try again. Children can be immunised for life."

In an article in The Times *on the future of the theatre, he explained his concern with the current emphasis on outreach:*

> *"Logically speaking, however, there is no earthly reason why people who go to the theatre when they are young should necessarily continue to do so when they get old. We do not expect young customers at discos and Nintendo counters still to be there when they are 40. By the same token, a theatre full of 12-year-olds who wear pleats and browse through the FT is not really a theatre for young people at all. It's educational in the worst sense: a training ground to duplicate the attitudes and conventions of today's middlebrow theatre audiences. If young people are attracted to theatres principally because they are future adults, theatre will inevitably become an increasingly middle-aged art form."*

Stephen Daltry, former Director of the Royal Court Theatre in London, believes that the key to building new younger audiences is to give them a topic that directly relates to them. He sees no reason why a young Afro-Caribbean audience would be interested in a play about having a mid-life crisis in Highgate. The Royal Court strives to present plays that directly speak to the experience of younger audiences. They also try to make attending the theatre be as informal and spontaneous as attending the cinema.

Source: Morris, 1995.

The Experience Generation

Life used to be a linear pattern of birth, school, job, marriage, family, retirement and death. But with increased longevity, life-long learning opportunities and new marriage and family patterns, the linear pattern no longer exists. This is a result of the Baby Boomer generation born after World War II. This large generational group grew up in a time of plenty, when anything seemed possible. They have been setting their own rules rather than acceding to the rules of authority. They also believe that ageing does not have to change their preferences.

Because they want control of their own destiny, they are impatient with passive experiences (Dychtwald, 2003). They want to participate actively in recreational and leisure activities, rather than just observe. For the arts, this means that passive experiences without a means for audience involvement will not attract. While museums have led the way in providing interactive exhibits for children, all cultural organisations will need to consider how to involve the culture consumer in the experience of participating in the arts. They are no longer content to be just an audience member.

This new experience-seeking generation tends to define themselves by the experiences they have had, not by their job title or family connection. Therefore, they are attracted to products that provide an experience in which they can participate (Hill, 2002). Here, cultural organisations have a particular advantage. They have always offered an arts experience. Now, they must create a means for the audience to feel involved with the experience. And this cannot be a lecture given by an expert to a passive audience.

The culture consumer differs not just because of their attendance patterns for the arts. Their value system and approach to life also differ. And these differences will remain with them as they age.

Competitor Analysis Worksheet

List three organisations your customers view as your competitors:

1.

2.

3.

Visit them and then use the table below to list what they offer that you don't:

Marketing Mix Factor	What Our Competitors Offer that We Don't
Products – availability, quality, benefits?	
Pricing – level, specials, variations?	
Customer service – attitude, ideas, services?	
Location – convenience, access, parking?	
Promotion – amount, types, creativeness?	
Purchase method – convenience, location?	

After you have studied the competition, use the scale below to rank yourself in comparison to what else is available to your customers. Now you know what you need to improve.

Overall Product Attractiveness

Excellent   *Poor*

1 2 3 4 5 6 7 8 9 10

Promotional Effectiveness

Excellent   *Poor*

1 2 3 4 5 6 7 8 9 10

Acceptable Pricing Level

Excellent   *Poor*

1 2 3 4 5 6 7 8 9 10

Suitable Distribution

Excellent   *Poor*

1 2 3 4 5 6 7 8 9 10

References

Abercrombie, N. and Longhurst, B. (1998) *Audiences: A Sociological Theory of Performance and Imagination*, Sage.

Baltic Contemporary Art Centre (2004) online at Baltic.mill.com.

Bambarger, B. (2004) "What is the Future of Classical Music" *Billboard Magazine* online at www.orchestrax.org/billboard.

Barbieri, S.M. (1998) "Orchestra X" in *Arts Reach*, October.

Brown, A. (2003) "Classical Music Consumer Segmentation Study: How Americans Relate to Classical Music and Their Local Orchestras" in *Arts Reach*, January.

Bruckman, A. (1999) "Cyberspace is not Disneyland: The Role of the Artist in a Networked World" in *Epistemology and the Learning Group: MIT Media Lab*, online at www.ahip.getty.edu/cyberpub.

Dychtwald, M. (2003) *Cycles: How We Will Live, Work and Buy*, The Free Press.

Fanciullo, D. (1998/99) "Innovative Educational Efforts Target Teenagers, Families, and Visually and Hearing-Impaired Youngsters" in *Arts Reach*, December/January.

Hill, S. (2002) *60 Trends in 60 Minutes*, Wiley.

Jupp, B. and Lawson, G. (1997) *Values Added: How Emerging Values Could Influence the Development of London*, London Arts Board and the London Planning Advisory Committee, London.

McElvoy, A. (1998) "Tiaras and Trainers can Mix at the Opera" in *Independent on Sunday*, October 18.

Morris, T. (1995) "Reaching Out to the Future" in London: *The Times*, January 8.

National Endowment for the Arts, *Research Division Report #36*, online at: http://arts.endow.gov/pub/Researcharts/Summary36.html.

New York City Opera (2004) "Big Deal" online at www.nycopera.com

Nichols, B. (2003) *Demographic Characteristics of Arts Attendance, 2002, Note #82*, National Endowment for the Arts.

Truskot, J. (1999) "Audience Development: Defined" in *Arts Reach*, April.

Chapter Four

MARKETING'S FUNCTION IN THE ORGANISATION

Marketing is still too often thought of by cultural organisations as trying to manipulate someone into buying something they do not want. Because marketing developed as a business tool, they feel it is tainted by corporate greed. But, of course, goods and services have been sold or exchanged between individuals long before there were corporations with marketing departments. Since marketing consists of making goods and services attractive and then communicating their availability to potential customers, most artists have always marketed. Artists have always needed someone to purchase their product, and marketing was used when artists tried to make what they produced attractive to those who might purchase. If artists did not wish to make the product attractive to buyers, they at least used marketing to communicate that their art was available.

The practice of marketing simply takes this basic human behaviour and plans its conception and implementation. The definition used by the American Marketing Association describes marketing as:

> "the process of planning and executing the conception, pricing, promotion, and distribution of ideas, goods, and services to create exchanges that satisfy individual and organisational goals" (Bennett, 1995).

It is interesting to note that the definition calls for an exchange that satisfies *both* the individual and the organisation. Marketing was never conceived as a means to seduce the individual into behaviour in which they did not wish to engage. There would be no long-term gain for any organisation in doing so. Likewise, the definition does not call for the organisation to satisfy the individual at any organisational cost. It is a negotiated exchange where a two-way dialogue takes place.

As part of this dialogue, first an exchange of information on desires and the means to fulfil them takes place. Individuals make their desires known and the organisation makes their product known. The individual may wish to modify their desires, if there is no organisation that can meet them, and the organisation may wish to modify their product, if it does not meet the needs of the potential customer.

It is also interesting to note that the definition describes marketing as the "conception" of ideas, goods or services. This part of the marketing definition, the idea that the marketing department decides upon which product to produce, is the part to which cultural organisations often object. They cite it as the reason why marketing is inappropriate and as the major difference between a corporate, profit-making organisation and a cultural non-profit organisation.

"Is Art Good For Us?"

Such a heretical question is actually the title of a book that examines this exact question. In it, Joli Jensen, the author, discusses the difference between high art and popular culture and how we came to believe that, rather than change the art product, we could change the consumer:

> *"When the arts are simply imagined to be beacons of excellence, to be created by a few for the edification of the many, they are clearly distinct from other, more popular forms. Current commentators may struggle with exactly how to determine the differences between them, based on content characteristics, but they insist on the need to prevent true art from being diluted, and to ensure that people have the training they obviously need to discern the best from the worst. . . . What commentators hope is that, with the right kinds of arts education, the populace will finally know enough to appreciate the wonderfulness of the arts they currently disdain, mistrust, or are bored by. They will come to like the right kind of art, and thus be able to enjoy the benefits such arts are presumed to bestow."*

Source: Jensen, 2002.

RELATIONSHIP BETWEEN MANAGEMENT & MARKETING

Management, as well as marketing, are relatively new fields of study compared with other academic disciplines. The seminal book on the subject, *The Practice of Management*, was written by Peter Drucker, an American, in the 1950s. Drucker was the first author to describe management as a distinct function of the organisation (Drucker, 1959). He was also one of the first to describe creating satisfied customers as the purpose of a business. The previous definition had been that the purpose of a business was making a profit. This was easy to accomplish in the US during the post-war consumer boom of the late 1940s and early 1950s, when there was a great demand for consumer goods. High consumer demand allowed companies to ignore Drucker's belief and little emphasis was placed on marketing.

However, during the 1960s, US companies became capable of manufacturing more products than were actually needed by the existing customer base. As a result, companies producing consumer goods became obsessed with competing with each other for customers. The goal was not satisfying customers, but rather to produce products that were in some way different from the products of their competitors. A company would seek to gain additional customers by first differentiating their product and then attempting to out-spend their competitors on marketing this difference to consumers. The focus on what the customer actually wanted, originally advocated by Drucker, was absent. During this period, the role of the marketing department was simply to help the company reach its profitability goals.

In the 1970s, companies became focused on overall strategic planning. The marketing function wasn't seen as central to a company's success, but only as one component of its overall strategy. It needs to be remembered that, at that time, most US managers had a common shared experience. They had been in military service in some form during the Second World War and, after their return to civilian life, they continued to use military concepts of organisation and an emphasis on top-down planning in their jobs. As a result, strategic planning departments, which produced thick organisational manuals containing detailed one- to five-year company plans, were common in the business world.

This approach worked successfully, because of the growth of the US economy and the lack of competition from companies in other countries that were still recovering from the war. When these companies again started manufacturing, they quickly geared up to also produce consumer goods. Besides meeting the consumer needs of their own citizens, they started to export and sell their products in the US. It was the inability of many major American industries to sell their products in the face of increased competition from abroad that showed the flaws in the marketing approach they were using. The strategic planning approach of management therefore fell into disrepute and strategic planning departments were disbanded (Schnaars, 1998).

By the mid-1980s, the focus of marketing was finally on Drucker's original concept of pleasing customers rather than just beating competitors. As a result, companies now started to place emphasis on researching what features and benefits the consumer desired so that the company could provide them in their products.

American companies had finally become focused on providing the product features and benefits consumers wanted. However during the 1980s, Japanese companies were intent on providing even more to American consumers. Japanese companies exporting to the US focused on superior quality, a feature American consumers had not asked for, because they did not even know that such a level of quality was possible, let alone available. This demonstrates the flaw in the traditional marketing concept that states that marketing should determine what the customer wants in a product. Because, when asked, customers can only answer with the features and benefits with which they are already familiar; they cannot describe the unknown. This poses a unique challenge for cultural organisations that provide benefits of which many consumers are unaware because they have never experienced the product.

Online Arts Marketing Advice

Now help is as close as the web for arts marketers. Thanks to the National Arts Marketing Project (NAMP), which has launched Arts Marketing Online (www.artsmarketing.org). The site, a project of the Arts & Business Council, Inc., shares arts marketing information and resources and allows everyone to benefit from the expertise and training of NAMP.

One of the unique features of the site is a forum room where arts managers and individual artists can post questions and share information. This extends the networking possibilities beyond the neighbouring organisations to anywhere in the world. In addition to getting information from peers, NAMP will also ask professional arts marketing consultants to log on to answer the questions posed.

You can also sign up for their free arts marketing newsletter sent out via email. So go online and sign up!

Source: Artsmarketing.org 2003.

PRODUCTS & CREATIVITY

In a cultural organisation, the idea, good or service is a given that exists first and is not conceived in order to simply have a product to market. Many believe that in a corporate, profit-making organisation, the organisation is formed first and then creates a product based solely on the needs and desires of the marketplace. But this is rarely the case. Most often the idea, good or service is a vision of a creative individual who then takes the idea to the marketplace. While the idea may be as mundane (to the cultural manager) as a new type of vacuum cleaner, to the creator it is just as visionary and creative as an artistic creation.

This point is made not to compare art to vacuum cleaners, but to demonstrate that the creation of products in the corporate world can be just as creative a process, driven by an individual vision, as in the arts world. The concept of marketing pertains to both the world of cultural organisations and corporate organisations; they are not as separate as they have been perceived.

Building a Better Mousetrap

Think inspiration, dedication and mission only apply to arts products? Think again!

In 1978, James Dyson noticed how the air filter in the paint spray-finishing room was constantly clogging with powder particles (just like a vacuum cleaner bag clogs with dust). So he designed and built an industrial cyclone tower, which removed the powder particles by centrifugal force, spinning the extracted air at the speed of sound. Could the same principle work in a vacuum cleaner?

James Dyson set to work. It took 5 years and 5,127 prototypes, until the world's first bagless vacuum cleaner from Dyson arrived.

Source: Dyson, 1999.

ARTS MANAGEMENT AS A PROFESSION

Cultural organisations have traditionally taken a negative view of marketing. The reasons include the belief that marketing is an inappropriate use of money and an unnecessary addition to overhead for cultural organisations that already have limited resources. There is also the negative preconception that marketing is both intrusive and manipulative and that using marketing strategy is a sell-out, which makes them no better than the profit-making businesses that sell popular culture. This view may result from the fact that the people who work in cultural organisations have specifically chosen not to work in the for-profit world.

The field of arts management as a distinct profession became popular in the 1970s. It developed out of the old role of the arts promoter whose job was to find a public audience for the artist, since the artist could no longer depend on individual patronage. This was not a partnership between artist and promoter; rather, it was the function of the promoter to serve the needs of the artist (Rentschler, 1998).

The growth of cultural organisations filled the need for a new type of intermediary. The new art administrators worked for the cultural organisation rather than directly for the artist, but their role was similar to that of the arts promoter: to serve the needs of the artist by finding an audience. For the cultural organisation, the criteria for success were achieving artistic goals, and financial rewards were considered to be of secondary importance. Therefore, art administration was seen as an appropriate area for women who had artistic interests, as the field was thought to lack the cut-throat competitive atmosphere of business management.

Rather than compete for profit, the role of the arts administrator was to allocate the resources from the state, to supervise the organisation and to ensure there was an audience for the artist. The primary focus was on the production of art, with the expectation there would be an audience willing to attend. Because the reason the organisation existed was first for the artistic product, second for the larger good of society, and only third for the consumer, unsurprisingly there was little emphasis on marketing. Little attention was given to the desires of the consumer, beyond considering how to arrange the art in a pleasing programme or exhibit.

The first comprehensive books on arts management were published in the US during this period. The focus on marketing at that time was only on promotion using advertising and subscription sales strategies. Most advertising was targeted to the middle-class and promoted attendance at cultural events as an important part of a middle-class lifestyle. The purpose of the subscription sales strategies was to encourage repeat customers to develop the value of loyalty to the cultural organisation (Rawlings-Jackson, 1996).

During the 1970s, the only focus on the customer, was the use of audience surveying to gather demographic information on who was attending the cultural event, so that marketing could attract more of the same audience. Little attention was paid to qualitative research to discover the motivation of the audience or to determine what the audience wanted. Instead, the focus was on demographic "bums-on-seats" research (Reiss, 1974).

By the 1980s, the rapid expansion of cultural organisations in the US resulted in too many organisations trying to attract a limited number of customers. As a result, the use of advertising simply to inform the public of the opportunities for attendance at culture events was no longer effective. The crowded arts marketplace resulted in a need for a more comprehensive marketing strategy.

They're Cheap, Easy and More is Better!

Who hasn't walked down an urban street and noticed the many posters, usually advertising popular culture events such as concerts and dance clubs. Would the same approach work for arts events?

A study conducted using university students in Montreal was designed to test whether the students exposed to such posters would be able to recall them later.

The results found that posters are an effective means to market arts events. In addition, they discovered that more is better. Recall was greatly increased, the more posters students were exposed to. And, if the posters were in the same location, recall increased even more.

And posters are cheap, which is good news for arts marketers on a budget! So get out the posters and hit the streets!

Source: Berneman and Kasparian, 2003.

Marketing and Audience Composition

Previously only the artistic director and the artist determined what culture the organisation would produce (Ní Bhrádaigh, 1997). The cultural product was then presented to the marketing director whose role was to use advertising to find a faceless but sufficient audience for the art. Since there was now no longer a sufficient number of customers, this division between the artistic and marketing functions started to break down. Both areas now discovered that they needed to understand the motivation and desires of the audience and why individuals chose to attend. In an effort to gather this information, the results of demographic studies were now not just counted, but were also analysed.

As a result, the cultural organisations found that their audience was a rather one-dimensional, homogeneous group of those who were well-educated, high income and primarily of the majority ethnic culture. Since the original purpose of the arts organisation was to present art that they considered to be indispensable to everyone, this was not good news. Cultural organisations had argued for public funding because art was necessary to nourish the soul and improve the values of the population as a whole. If only a limited and narrow part of the population was attending, then it was difficult for cultural organisations to argue that they should receive public funding.

So the emphasis changed from filling seats to broadening the audience for the arts and, in the 1990s, various marketing efforts were tried. Since the arts administrator now knew that the arts were largely attended by those with high incomes, they concluded that people without high incomes did not attend because they could not afford to buy a ticket. Their marketing focus widened to include pricing. It was believed that attendance could be increased through special ticket concessions for low income people, including young people and seniors. Little notice appears to have been taken of the fact that these groups had the money to spend on other activities. After all, the young in particular are large consumers of expensive popular culture.

It did occur to cultural organisations that a significant portion of the population did not desire their product. If it did occur, it was also believed that this portion could be educated to understand and appreciate the arts. In an effort to educate everyone to appreciate the arts, outreach programmes became an increasingly important focus for cultural organisations. While these programmes were good public relations, there was no evidence that they were the answer to attendance problems (Kolb, 2002).

By the turn of the century, external changes finally forced cultural organisations to rethink their mission and product, rather than only focus on increasing attendance through promotion and pricing. With a rapidly changing society, many cultural organisations are no longer sure of having a future audience. This period of change can be seen as an opportunity as it necessitates the need for cultural organisations to rethink the relationship between themselves and the wider society. In fact, periods of change often make people more open to accepting new ideas (Bridges, 2003).

Country Music + Classical Music = Nashville?

Everyone thinks of the country music recording industry when they think of Nashville. And that's OK with the Nashville Symphony's Executive Director, Alan Valentine. While other orchestras struggle, in December 2003, the Nashville Symphony broke ground on a new concert hall right near the Country Music Hall of Fame.

Is this an "image" problem for the Symphony? No way! In fact Valentine explained,

> *"The manager of the Country Music Hall of Fame and I have been doing a lot of talking because we are going to be neighbors. We've been dreaming of the day when we can have huge music festivals in the park right outside our front doors . . . We tend to put things in boxes and say this is country and this is classical music and this is gospel. There is all kinds of potential for creative collaborations that are hard to imagine right now. Music is music, and if it's good, it's good, and if it's not it's not."*

Source: Stone, 2003.

DEVELOPMENT OF MARKETING THEORY

While originally marketing was thought of as only useful for physical products, companies soon learned that marketing could be applied not just to products but also to services. During the 1980s demand for services such as tourism, transportation and financial services were growing as the general level of income in the population rose. Those managing the service industries thought that they, too, could use marketing theory and practice to inform customers about their service products. They first used the same approach of differentiating their products from the products offered by their competitors, rather than focusing on customer needs, that consumer goods business had already mistakenly followed.

The cultural industries are part of the service sector, so it is not surprising that they also became interested in marketing. But most cultural organisations lagged behind profit-making organisations in adopting marketing strategy. This may have been because reliance on public funding shielded them from worrying about revenue from customers. Therefore cultural organisations had less interest in applying all aspects of marketing theory.

The "Four Ps"

The standard marketing concept of analysing the strategy for selling a product in terms of the "Four Ps" of *price, product, place* and *promotion* was popularised in the 1981 book, *Basic Marketing: A Managerial Approach* by E. J. McCarthy. This marketing concept is still used although some have expanded the "Ps" to include *presentation* and *people* for services. The concept stresses the importance for the marketing department to analyse the product by all the "Ps" not just promotion in creating their marketing strategy.

Buying Art Interest Free

It is difficult to imagine a business offering expensive products that does not offer credit. Everyone is accustomed to paying by instalment for large purchases but galleries still expect people to be wealthy enough so that price and payment are not an issue when purchasing an original. The Arts Council of England has now made it easier to purchase contemporary art through Artloan. The programme pays participating galleries up-front for the art. The purchaser then repays the loan using a standing order, interest free, over a 10-month period. From £100 to £2,000 can be borrowed over a one-year period after a simple credit check, which is completed at the time of purchase.

Perhaps it's time other cultural organisations were able to say, "Will that be cash, cheque, credit card or loan?"

Source: Arts Council of England, 2003.

Cultural Organisations and the One "P"

When cultural organisations became interested in marketing, they first focused on promotion. Since cultural organisations had a mission that already defined their *product*, they would not consider changing their product line to attract new customers. Because cultural organisations were subsidised, the *price* they charged was already below cost and probably could not be further reduced to attract customers. Cultural organisations were also often restricted to the *place* where they presented their art. As a result, *promotion* was the main marketing focus for cultural organisations.

The promotion aspect of marketing was usually handled by broadcasting a message via the mass media on the product's features, which is the traditional mass marketing approach to selling. Since, at that time, marketing departments had less access to information about their customers, all they could do was assume that everyone was a potential consumer. The result was a marketing message based on what the producer thought any potential consumer ought to know.

The Other "Ps"

The marketing of culture by cultural organisations must now move beyond focusing only on a use of promotion. They must accept that they are now competing with not only other cultural organisations, but also other forms of entertainment and leisure activity. To develop a marketing strategy that will not only help them to survive, but also to succeed in the face of this competition, cultural organisations must produce a product that provides the benefits that the consumer wants, even if part of this benefit is to be entertained. This product must also be competitively priced and conveniently placed.

Cultural organisations need to stop thinking of entertainment as a bad word. In today's highly competitive global workplace, consumers are working longer hours. In their leisure time, understandably they want a way to relax. Cultural organisations should remember that the word "entertain" also means to beguile, delight, enthral, divert, charm and absorb. A cultural organisation should not be ashamed of providing these qualities, while they also provide art that challenges and stimulates people to think and feel in new ways.

The Arts & Marketing: A Changing Relationship

How did the relationship between cultural organisations and marketing change over the last 30 years?

The Foundation Period (1974–84) was shaped by the need for cultural organisations to change their attitude toward marketing and was characterised by a desire to learn about their customers. The organisations were also starting to realise the important role the marketing mix played in their success in attracting an audience. Characteristics of marketing issues in the foundation period included:

- *Learning to apply marketing concepts.*
- *Educating visitors about product.*
- *Selling focus.*
- *Reliance on demographic studies.*
- *Marketing implications of decisions ignored.*
- *Activity mix.*

The Professionalisation Period (1985–94) saw a new understanding that the cultural organisation's future was tied to success in the marketplace. During this period, "gate-keeper" management was replaced with entrepreneurial management. Characteristics of marketing issues in the professional period included:

- *Strategy-driven, action-oriented studies.*
- *Marketing implications of decisions considered.*
- *Marketing focus.*
- *Increased use of psychographic studies.*
- *Various marketing models offered.*
- *Marketing mix.*

And now? Arts marketers understand that marketing is the "process" of developing the relationship between the product and the customer. It's ongoing and involves everyone in the organisation.

Source: Rentschler, 1998, Artsmarketing.org, 2004.

MARKETING FOCUS

Basic marketing theory states that the company needs to find the right customer and then present the product to the customer in the right way. There are three basic methods of how to market products:

- Production focus
- Sales focus
- Consumer focus.

The production focus view holds that a good product will bring in customers on its own. If the company develops the right product, it will have customers. The sales view is that any product can be sold, if the company has the right sales strategy. The consumer focus accepts the need to consider the desires of the consumer.

Production Focus

The production method of marketing looks inward, to what the organisation can produce. The organisation determines what its employees are capable of producing and bases its production decision on their capabilities. For example, in a for-profit company, the question might be what the engineers can design. In a cultural organisation, the question might be what type of opera the singers can sing. Of course, company employees are not likely to refuse to produce a new product, while an opera singer may well object to singing an opera of which they are capable, but in which they are not interested.

If the people employed in the organisation are capable of producing more than one product, the decision as to what to produce is left to the people involved in the production. Despite its very business-sounding name, the production focus is historically the approach that has been taken by most cultural organisations. It is an approach where the capabilities and desires of those involved in the organisation come first.

If the organisation has sufficient funding or there happens to be a demand for the product, the cultural organisation will succeed. Unfortunately if there is insufficient funding or demand for the product, the organisation will fail. If there are other organisations offering the same cultural product, the demand may be insufficient for both organisations and the less favoured organisation, or both, will fail.

Because having insufficient consumer demand results in insufficient revenue, which leaves the organisation dependent on public funding, the production focus is a dangerous route for any cultural organisation to take. This reliance on public funding allows the organisation to produce the cultural product of their choice without concern for the marketplace. In this case, the cultural organisation measures success by the amount of cultural product they produce, not by meeting attendance or revenue goals. Since the organisation is a culture-producing entity that wishes to produce culture, it is happy to oblige with more.

Tips from the Big Guys

Group sales are a major source of income for theatres booking long running popular musicals. For a block-buster, such as Disney's The Lion King, *they account for between 25 and 35 per cent of capacity. How do they do it? They rely on an entire infrastructure of booking agencies, along with group sales to organisations and tourist companies.*

While smaller theatres cannot match their budgets, they can use some of their techniques. Group sales managers for large theatres know that they must reach the information source. For the tourist or business traveller, this is often the hotel or tourism office staff. These staff members are asked for advice on where and what to attend. By providing the staff with information and even free tickets, they can be influenced as to what advice they give to others. By inviting them to performances, even if they cannot or do not attend, a personal relationship is built with them.

Use of such marketing techniques will not make a bad event a success. But it is estimated that, in the theatre world, careful marketing can turn a show running at a borderline 60 to 70 per cent capacity into a success.

Are there any groups in your town that might be interested in attending if they received a discount?

Source: Benedict, 1998.

Sales Focus

A second method of marketing is the sales focus that emphasises selling the product and in which success is measured by the number of products sold and the amount of revenue received. Some cultural organisations often have the unfortunate idea that the sales method is the only approach to marketing. In fact, it is an approach taken by only a small number of businesses. The sales focus assumes that consumers can be convinced to purchase by using an aggressive sales technique. This approach is usually not successful, as most people are very savvy consumers, and the approach wrongly tries to dictate to the consumer rather than listen to what they desire. Many organisations that fail after pursuing a production focus, then adopt the sales focus in an effort to boost sales and save their organisation.

Consumer Focus

Today, the consumer focus is considered contemporary marketing theory. This method is based on creating a product that first meets the needs and desires of the consumer. This does not mean that the organisation's capabilities and desires are ignored. No organisation can meet the needs of the consumer by providing a product it does not have the capabilities or desire to produce. Of course, a mission-centred cultural organisation will also have limits on how much, if any, it can change its cultural product to meet the needs of the consumer. Nevertheless, it is possible to keep within these limits, without becoming reliant on the production focus, where only the cultural organisation's capabilities and desires are considered.

There is room in the consumer focus approach for compromise between the desires of the consumers and those of the cultural organisation because each defines the product in a different way. For the cultural organisation, the product is the art product produced. But for the consumer, the product is the total package of experience including an evening's entertainment, a learning experience, a social experience, a yearly ritual and/or an adventurous event. All of these can be provided by the cultural organisation without changing the core cultural product. What would change would be the way the cultural product is communicated, presented and packaged. If the organisation is unwilling to consider any modification in these features, it is back to the production focus, where either a sufficient demand must exist or the cultural organisation must be subsidised.

Likewise, consumers understand that there are restraints on what a mission-centred organisation can produce and thus they are willing to modify their demands at any given price and product level. Many for-profit companies, such as organisations involved in marketing of environmental products, serve a wider purpose than merely satisfying consumer's needs. They communicate both their mission and product via marketing to consumers, who may even be willing to pay more, or forego some product benefits, to consume these socially beneficial products. For many of these organisations, professional marketing strategy is seen as a useful tool and not as something in opposition to the mission of the organisation.

Advice Doesn't Have to Be Serious

How does an orchestra survive in a small, rural Pennsylvanian town? By making sure that everyone knows they are welcome, whoever they are and whatever their interests – and by reminding them not to take classical music so seriously. One of ways the Williamsport Symphony Orchestra gets this across is through their website's FAQ section. An example:

Question: "What should I wear to a symphony concert?"

Answer: "It's generally a good idea to wear something – too much nudity in the audience distracts the attention from the orchestra, and the musicians' egos are easily bruised. Beyond that, just relax and remember the dress code of the third millennium: 'If you bought a ticket, you're appropriately dressed.' (Shoes and shirts are required.)"

Source: Boerckel, 2004.

Changing the Marketing Focus

It is not easy for a cultural organisation to switch from a production or sales focus to a consumer focus approach. The change too often only comes about when the organisation has lost customers and is facing financial difficulties. This crisis is the start of the solution and may lead to a change in the entire manner in which the organisation views itself and does business. But, instead of facing difficult questions about their identity and mission, cultural organisations too often continue to fall back on the argument that their existence should be subsidised because it is in society's best long-term interests.

What cultural organisations need to understand is that every product faces competition. The problem is that cultural organisations have not understood what the competition is for cultural events. Defined narrowly, the competing product for cultural events is other cultural events. Defined broadly, it would be any leisure activity, including cinema, sports events and staying home with a rented DVD.

While price is one issue in choosing a product, it is usually the deciding issue only when comparing very similar products. Too many cultural organisations believe that the affordability of tickets is the key to increasing attendance. However if the competing product is another leisure activity, price may only be a small consideration as consumers are willing to pay a considerable amount of money on leisure.

Two Performances: Onstage and in the Audience

At any cultural event, there are actually two performances taking place. One is onstage and the other is happening in the audience. When consumers purchase tickets, it is for the opportunity to observe both the onstage performance and also to participate in the audience performance. They desire the opportunity to interact with other audience members as a means to start and develop social relationships with individuals they consider to be of a desirable social class.

For many, the performance is a means, not an end. Therefore, the consumer's perception of the anticipated audience will either attract or repel them. Advertising must explicitly or implicitly carry this information.

Source: Gainer, 1993.

CULTURAL INSTITUTIONS & MARKETING

In summary, it is a major concern for those managing cultural organisations that, for many art forms, both in Europe and in the US, audience attendance is both ageing and declining while more arts organisations are competing for attendance. This decline in audience demand is of concern as it decreases ticket revenue and, even more importantly, makes it increasingly difficult to justify public funding.

As a result, there has been an increasing awareness amongst cultural organisations of the need to develop the future audience for art and culture. Whilst culture may be considered "timeless," social changes have resulted in cultural consumers with very different needs and priorities than the current patrons of cultural organisations. These different needs and priorities must be addressed if there is to be an audience in the future.

Marketing for cultural organisations needs to be re-examined even more now that the distinction between popular culture and high culture has become less well-defined. The cultural product needs to be re-defined and re-positioned because the competitors of high culture are no longer only other similar cultural programming, but instead, other cultural and entertainment events from both Western and non-Western cultures.

The potential audience for culture has to be re-thought now that people are working harder and longer due to global competition. The leisured middle-class was the target market for most cultural organisations, but the era when people could work only a short seven-hour day and, therefore, still have the energy for a challenging concert on a weekday evening is drawing to a close, if it is not already gone. Also, in an era when technology provides us with information in ever quicker and shorter formats, it is time for cultural organisations to reconsider how culture is presented to the public and why culture is presented in its current format.

In today's rapidly changing marketplace, where technology creates entirely new products and provides new distribution systems for old products, even businesses have to develop new marketing strategies. If for-profit businesses are re-examining how to market products, it is even more important for cultural organisations to re-examine the role of marketing for the arts.

There will always be a market segment that desires traditional high culture presented in the traditional format by traditional cultural organisations. The few large and well-known providers of high culture whose reputation for stars and quality provides them with brand name recognition will be the organisations of choice for this market segment. The remaining cultural organisations will need to develop marketing strategies that can help them survive, and even thrive, in the new cultural marketplace by targeting the new culture consumer.

Marketing Audit Worksheet

Before you start to develop your marketing strategy based on product, price, place and promotion, it's important to examine your current marketing. What has worked should be continued. What has not – should be stopped. Don't waste your time and money!

Current Plan	*Describe*	*Has it worked?*
New products		
Pricing strategies		
Improved venues		
Distribution methods		
Advertising		
Sales incentives		
Personal selling		
Public relations		
Direct marketing		

Our current marketing goal(s): (Increase attendance? Launch new products? Attract new audiences? Beat the competition?)

References

Arts Council of England (2003) online at www.artscouncil.org.uk/funding/buyingart_howto.html.

Artsmarketing.org (2004) "Basic Marketing Strategy" in *Practical Lessons in Marketing*, online at www.artsmarketing.org/tutorials

Benedict, D. (1998) "Theatre: How Do They Do That? What Transforms a Mere Musical into a Blockbuster?" in *Independent*, December 9.

Bennett, P.D. (1995) *Dictionary of Marketing Terms*, American Marketing Association.

Berneman, C. and Kasparian, M. (2003) "Promotion of Cultural Events through Urban Postering: An Exploratory Study of its Effectiveness" in *International Journal of Arts Management*, Fall.

Bhrádaigh, E. Ní (1997) "Arts Marketing: A Review of Research and Issues" in *From Maestro to Manager: Critical Issues in Arts & Culture Management*, Oak Tree Press.

Boerckel, G. (2004) "Mostly Honest Answers to Pointed Questions About the WSO" online at www.williamsportsymphony.com/faq.

Bridges, W. (2003) *Managing Transitions: Making the Most of Change*, Perseus Publishing.

Drucker, P. (1959) *The Practice of Management*: Reissue Edition (1993), Harper Business.

Dyson Corporation website (1999) online at: http://www.dyson.com/story03, September.

Gainer, B.J. (1993) "An Empirical Investigation of the Role of the Involvement with a Gendered Product", *Psychology and Marketing* Vol. 10, No. 4.

Jensen, J. (2002) *Is Art Good for Us? Beliefs about Culture in American Life*, Rowman & Littlefield.

Kolb, B. (2002) "The Effect of Generational Change on Classical Music Concert Attendance and Orchestras' Responses in the UK and US" in *Cultural Trends*, Issue 41, 2001.

Rawlings-Jackson, V. (1996) *Where Now? Theatre Subscription Selling in the 90's, A Report on the American Experience*, Arts Council of England.

Reiss, A. (1974) *The Arts Management Handbook*, Law-Arts Publishers.

Rentschler, R. (1998) "Museums and Performing Arts Marketing: A Climate of Change" in *The Journal of Arts Management, Law & Society*, Spring, Vol. 28, Issue 1.

Schnaars, S.P. (1998) *Marketing Strategy: Customers & Competition*, The Free Press.

Stone, M. (2003) "Nashville Symphony to Break Ground for Multimillion-Dollar Concert Hall: A Mega-Scale Collaboration for Music City and the Symphony" in *ArtsReach*, March.

Chapter Five

Consumer Motivation & Choice

A major problem for cultural organisations is that both the middle class, which has been the mainstay of the cultural audience, and the new culture consumer, no longer lead the more leisured life-style that they did just a few years ago. The reasons are many, and include increased work hours due to global competition and industry mergers, longer commuting time, two career families, and extra-curricular activities of children. The result is that people are working much longer hours and experiencing more stress in their lives. The desire to experience art may be concealed by the desire just to get home and collapse on the sofa. If consumers today have less time and energy, it is obvious that they will need to be highly motivated to attend a cultural event. Therefore to motivate attendance, the cultural event must be packaged to provide additional benefits than only experiencing art.

Reasons for Attendance

To develop a successful strategy for attracting consumers to cultural events, it is important to understand why people choose to attend. The literature on attendance at cultural events gives a variety of possibilities that fall into four broad categories:

- Interest in a particular art form or artist.
- Desire for leisure/entertainment.
- Participation in social ritual.
- Self-improvement.

Those with an interest in a particular art form or artist are probably already attending. Understanding the other possible reasons for attendance is necessary if promotion is to be successful.

Leisure & Entertainment

Rather than a specific interest in a particular art form or artist, for many consumers attending a play, concert or visiting a museum is only one of many possible alternatives that could be chosen as a means to fill their leisure time. The benefits they seek – relaxation, entertainment and an opportunity to socialise with friends and family – are the same benefits that would be provided by other leisure activities.

Why Do People Attend?

A survey conducted of theatre-goers in France determined that there are three main motives for attending the theatre:

- *Educational: Cultural "meat", learning from the performance.*
- *Intellectual stimulation: Personal development, an intellectual challenge.*
- *Pleasure: Social, interaction, communication.*

The cultural event must meet at least one of these needs to attract an audience. Unfortunately, cultural organisations too often focus on the first two motives and not the third. To attract a larger audience, the organisation needs to use "add-ons" to meet the socialisation and communication needs of the audience. This could be done through social hours before or after the performance, cultural trips to places associated with the art form and opportunities to meet and interact with the artists. The researchers also concluded that the publicity used by the organisations must focus on all three motives and not just on the programming. Advertisements that only focus on the work and the artist do not speak to the socialisation needs of the potential audience.

Source: Bouder-Pailler, 1999.

Social Ritual

Another motive for consumers to attend a cultural event is the opportunity to participate in a form of social ritual. While the consumer may also desire the same benefits sought by those who merely chose a cultural event as an entertainment option, they also desire something more. For the traditional high art audience, attendance may be an affirmation of their social values (Small, 1987). The fact that the art was created by an artist who lived long ago and yet is still appreciated, is seen as confirmation that effort will be rewarded, even if belatedly, and that triumph over difficulty is always possible. These are core values of the middle-class. The art, therefore, provides a proof of the stability of middle-class values in a rapidly changing world. Of course, this emphasis on hard work and self-control may not be attractive to consumers who might be looking for relaxation, amusement and socialisation (Blake, 1997).

The Concert Hall Has Never Been Just a Place to Hear Music

The association of the performance of classical music with the upper levels of society developed early and remains true today. Starting in the beginning of the 19th century, classical music was performed in elegant special-purpose halls designed to be very different from the other public places where music was performed, such as taverns and coffee-houses. The concert halls were to give the illusion that the audience members all came from a class where sumptuous surroundings were taken for granted.

The rituals on how the musicians and audience should behave in the concert hall were developed as a means to reinforce class distinctions. These rituals were very important to the upper-middle-class members of the audience as it was the means by which they sought to distance themselves from those lower in the social hierarchy and to associate themselves with those higher. Unfortunately, this is sometimes still true today.

Source: Small, 1996.

Self-improvement

Almost all art appreciation books stress self-improvement as a motive for attendance at cultural events. But this self-improvement must be achieved through hard work and pain, not enjoyment. In the music appreciation book, *Who's Afraid of Classical Music?*, learning to enjoy classical music is compared to body building: no pain, no gain (Walsh, 1989). The book explains that popular music is popular because it is easy, but the author advises now that the reader is older, it is time to put aside the things of childhood. Readers are now ready to learn to enjoy "sophisticated" music, if only they are willing to work hard to do so.

Letters to a Musical Boy

The theme of self-improvement continues through most old and new art appreciation books. In Letters to a Musical Boy, *written back in 1940, the author explains the difficulty inherent in appreciating good music.*

> *"And so John, we have come to the end of our discussion. If you have learned anything from what we have discussed, it will, I hope, encourage you to explore further this universal language of music, either as a listener or, if you possibly can, as a performer, even if it is only as a member of a village choir or local orchestra. You will have realised, perhaps, how great are your opportunities; but I hope that you may meet difficulties as well. For music is not an easy art either to practise or to enjoy. True enjoyment means something very much more than turning on a switch and sinking back into an arm-chair. To some, music may only be a pleasant pastime; but to others, it is a spiritual experience. The more difficulties you overcome in the search for it, the greater your rewards."*

Source: Bruxner, 1940.

CONSUMER DECISION-MAKING

When making decisions about products, consumers consider the benefits they will receive from the product *versus* the cost of the product. Value is the relationship between the satisfaction the benefits provide and the cost the consumer must pay including the ticket price, transportation, childcare and any other related expenses. However, even if there is no charge for attendance or other monetary costs, there is still the cost to the customer in time and effort when they attend.

When designing promotions, cultural organisations often do not mention value, because they assume everyone already understands that the benefit of experiencing the art outweighs any monetary or other cost to the consumer. If cultural organisations do consider value, they often only focus on communicating the availability of low-priced tickets.

While it is true that price and other costs are important to most consumers, costs are not the only factor when assessing value. Consumers also consider the entire package of benefits they will receive from attending. Cultural organisations often assume that their audience is attending only because of the quality of art and do not understand that they must also communicate to consumers that the quality of the experience as a whole will meet their expectations.

Consumer Definition of Quality

The cultural organisation's mission is to produce culture of the highest quality, and therefore it often believes that consumer satisfaction only depends on the quality of the art. But consumers, who are understandably less educated on the fine points of the art form, may have other expectations that define quality. While the standard of the art is important, consumers will also make a decision to attend based on the quality of the entire experience. This will include their expectations in regard to such factors as the ambience of the venue, the convenience of the location, the additional amenities provided and the quality of the customer service they receive. What factors are included in the definition of the quality of the experience can only be defined by the consumer. The cultural organisation can provide a quality experience only by meeting or exceeding expectations that result from this consumer definition of quality.

The consumer brings these expectations of what they will receive as part of a quality experience to the purchase process. These expectations are often influenced by word-of-mouth recommendations from friends and relatives, from the media or from past personal experience. In fact, an important component for the consumer when judging quality is how they are treated at the venue. They will assess the quality of the experience starting from when they enter the venue's front door. It is often the lowest paid employee or volunteer who has the most impact on consumers' perceptions of quality.

Rather than Just Opening the Door – Build a Bridge

How do you build bridges between the cultural institution and the community to increase attendance? Not by just telling the public why they should come. Instead, a report put out by the National Endowment for the Arts suggests the following:

"Take stock of the cultural resources that already exist, paying particular attention to those pockets of creativity – in the community center, the senior-citizen home, places of worship and the like – that might have been overlooked in previous inventories. In what ways are Americans already participating in the arts, and how can this involvement be increased?

Find ways to provide forums for some of the new voices in the community. What are the barriers to access and involvement in the arts, and how can they be overcome?

Make an effort to balance the needs of the professional arts sector with efforts to involve citizens more directly in the arts, through a range of outreach, educational and participatory activities. How can cultural services be delivered in the same way that other community needs – health care, education, and public safety, for example – are met?

Instead of simply inviting citizens to attend the arts, find new ways in which artists and arts organizations can bring art to the people, interacting with the public outside of the concert hall and museum."

Source: Larson, 1996.

Maslow's Hierarchy of Needs

Maslow's hierarchy of needs is a theory that describes how a person's life circumstances motivate them to fill internal needs, only one of which is the need to experience culture (Maslow, 1987). In this theory, the strongest motivator is to satisfy the immediate physiological or human needs for food, clothing and shelter to keep body and soul together. After these needs are met, the individual can then focus on safety or on ensuring that these needs will be met in the future. Once the basic needs of life have been secured for today and the future, individuals can then meet their social needs by associating with others. Once their social needs are met by associating with others, they then feel the contrary need to separate themselves from the group by gaining esteem, either as an individual, or as a member of a unique group. And after all these needs are met, individuals can then develop the unique nature of their inner selves through self-actualisation.

Maslow's Hierarchy of Needs

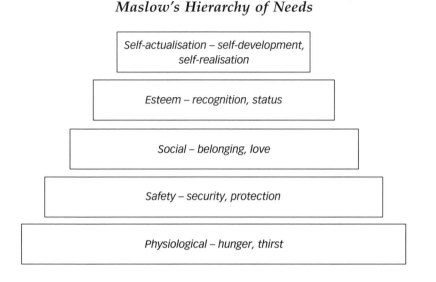

Maslow stated that these needs are satisfied in an ascending order. Lower order needs can be satisfied externally through factors such as food and drink, regular employment and family associations, while higher order needs are satisfied internally through feelings of self-worth. Individuals will be motivated to meet a need, but once the need is met, they will start to feel the next level need and seek to meet it. What is interesting is how the theory can be used to examine how cultural organisations view the public's need for culture.

The typical audience for culture usually consists of educated individuals with high incomes who are from the upper middle class or above. It can be assumed that these individuals have already met the lower order physiological, safety and social needs and the need for culture is felt only when these other lower-order needs have already been met.

Consuming Culture to Belong

The need to belong is at the heart of the buying and selling dynamic. By buying culture, people can become part of the creative process. They then, at least temporarily, belong to a group of other creative people.

An example of this need is the experience of the Lahti Orchestra in Finland. At the beginning of the 1990s, they were just one among many small provincial orchestras. They then discovered and recorded a CD of a previously unknown piece by Sibelius and decided to use the opportunity to change the way in which the orchestra was perceived.

Their new image was designed to include everyone from the conductor on down to the cleaning lady. Or perhaps it is more accurate to state that they understood that, in the mind of the community, the orchestra consists of everyone from the conductor to the cleaning lady.

They used the release of the CD to announce that they would now focus their programming on the work of Finnish composers. They explained their new "brand" image in newspaper advertisements. These adverts also explained that they wanted to be associated with the community and not separate from it. The community responded enthusiastically to supporting "their" orchestra.

Source: Morris, Degenhardt and Spreadbury, 1998 and Lahti Symphony, 2003.

Most cultural organisations believe that high culture improves and develops the human psyche (Woodmansee, 1994). However, except perhaps for a few rare individuals, people who are struggling with the basics of existence do not feel the need to use culture for a self-actualising experience because other, lower-order needs take precedence. Those few individuals who will ignore their basic needs in the pursuit of art often are artists themselves, or members of what was once termed the bohemian class and is now called the counter-culture. These individuals put the need to appreciate culture first, with other needs such as security, a regular job, and adequate income following lower in the scale. These individuals will then look down on members of the middle classes, whose appreciation is suspect since they have not sacrificed meeting any of their basic needs in order to enjoy culture.

This does not mean that individuals who are unable to take the time to participate in cultural activities, because they are busy satisfying lower-level needs, are unable to appreciate culture. It does mean that culture must be presented to them in a manner and setting that also helps to satisfy their other needs at the same time. This group may have no objection to self-esteem and self-actualisation, but they may want a cultural event they attend to also meet socialisation, and even physiological, needs.

Unfortunately, some people working in cultural organisations feel that supplying cultural events that meet lower level human needs somehow debases culture (Woodmansee, 1994). They have a traditional belief that culture should only be enjoyed for the higher reasons and culture that meets any other needs is suspect. This belief may exist because the original audience for culture consisted of the upper classes and nobility. Their place in society was defined by having the money that freed them from focusing on lower level needs and which allowed them to pursue cultural activities.

But if individuals can meet more than one need at the same time, there is no reason that self-esteem cannot grow and self-actualisation occur, even when other lower needs for sustenance and socialisation are being met. Cultural organisations can use this theory of human behaviour to understand how to make the presentation of culture attractive to a wider span of the population.

THE PURCHASE PROCESS

If the cultural organisation wishes to meet the quality expectations of the consumer, it must first understand how consumers make the decision to purchase. Understanding the process by which consumers make choices gives the cultural organisation an advantage in both designing a marketing strategy and positioning its product correctly. In the ideal world envisioned by the cultural organisation, the consumer recognises the need to participate in a specific cultural activity, such as visiting a museum or hearing a concert, and then simply chooses from the available cultural alternatives. This assumes that the main motivating factor for attendance is the cultural product, which may be true for culture enthusiasts but not for culture consumers.

An important part of understanding how to attract attendance is awareness of how the consumer engages in the purchase process. The five steps in the process start with need or problem recognition and continue through post-purchase evaluation.

The Purchase Process

Need or Problem Recognition

↓

Information Search

↓

Evaluation of Alternative Products

↓

Product Purchase

↓

Post-purchase Product Evaluation

Need or Problem Recognition

The process starts with consumers recognising that they have a need to fill or a problem to solve. The consumer's problem may be where to attend a cultural event that will show the visual art of a particular artist. Or it may be the problem of what to do while on holiday in a foreign city, how to relax after a long work-week, or how to meet attractive and interesting people. Of course, the cultural organisation's main mission is to present culture, but it must also recognise what additional problems it may be solving for their audience.

In reality, the problems that consumers need to solve may be as general as what to do for an evening's entertainment or as specific as the need to attend a cultural event with a client they wish to impress. However before the consumer can act, they must perceive that a problem even exists. Even the most avid supporter of culture will acknowledge that it is not felt as a primary need, such as food and shelter, by most people.

Information Search

The consumer next must initiate an information search to discover what potential activities are available that will meet their needs. The cultural organisation must ensure that the information it is providing is in a convenient form and place. Consumers must be able to find the necessary information at the time they are making the decision. It is also important to consider who is actually making the attendance choice. In any choice, there is someone who is the initiator of the process, but they may not be the person who is the ultimate attender.

If today's consumer is feeling stressed and over-worked, then it can be assumed that, even when they have recognised a need, they will have limited time to spend on the second step in the process, searching for information on how to meet the need. In addition, since hectic lifestyles do not allow for long-range planning of activities, the information needs to be available at the appropriate time, which is usually shortly before the event. Fortunately, technology provides the cultural organisation with new methods such as the Internet and email, which can be used to provide the consumer with information in a timely fashion.

People are Talking and Hopefully About You!

What is "buzz?" Buzz is a marketing term that refers to all the person-to-person communications about your cultural organisation and its product. Buzz spreads via phone, email, letters, at the copy machine and over the dinner table. When making the purchase decision, people are more likely today to rely on the recommendations of other people they know, rather than information contained in advertisements. Why? According to author Emanual Rosen, there are three reasons:

- *Customers can hardly hear you – today people are exposed to an avalanche of commercial messages.*
- *Customers are sceptical – they have been disappointed by the claims in commercial messages in the past.*
- *Customers are connected – they have new tools for sharing information.*

Source: Rosen, 2000.

Evaluation of Alternatives

After consumers have gathered sufficient information, they must then evaluate the available alternatives. The cultural organisation must understand for its targeted audience what are the most influential evaluative criteria. For some consumers, the criteria may be the quality of the art. For others, it could be as commonplace as the convenience of the location or the availability of parking.

So that consumers can make the decision between alternatives, they should be provided with information on the time, place and programme for the cultural event. However, they should also be given information on what other benefits will be provided. For example, consumers may want to know whether food will be available, so time can be saved and socialisation chances increased. For consumers with limited cultural knowledge, they need to know they will be provided with information about the performance or exhibit, which will help them to enjoy the experience.

Consumers must be able to obtain sufficient information on both costs and benefits for all the various opportunities so that they can make an informed decision on which choice to pursue. Consumers may ignore possible alternatives if the information is unavailable, because they do not have the time to risk participating in an activity that might not meet their needs.

Purchase

Cultural organisations often neglect to consider that, once consumers have made the decision, they must actually purchase the ticket to attend the event. The organisation must examine the ease with which the purchase transaction can be completed by the potential customer. In an age when everything can be purchased over the web, many cultural organisations still have consumers stand in line in the rain to get into their venue.

Post-purchase Evaluation

After the purchase, the final step in the process is that of the consumer performing a post-purchase evaluation. At this time, the consumer will decide whether their quality expectations have been met, or even exceeded, or whether they have been disappointed with the experience. The cultural organisation must remember that it is not enough just to get the audience in the door, they also must make sure that the audience's experience is of the quality expected and provides the desired benefits. Only if the consumer is satisfied that the event provided an acceptable solution to the initial need or problem will they choose to repeat the experience.

Let's Have a Party!

Rather than just send out a press release announcing the start of single ticket purchasing, the Toronto Symphony sent an invitation to a party.

"... Single ticket purchasers (as well as the curious)" were invited to stop by the concert hall. Besides being able to buy tickets, there were free CDs, a contest for a free transatlantic cruise for two and free lunch for ticket buyers. And the whole event was remote broadcast on the local classical music radio station.

How did they afford to host a party? The contest prize and lunches were donated (with prominent thanks being given to the sponsors), and the CDs were the symphony's own.

Source: Toronto Symphony, 2004.

CONSUMER MOTIVATION

When going through the decision making process, consumers are influenced by forces that are either internal (personal) or external (social). Internal forces include the consumer's values, the resulting beliefs and their own unique personality. The external social forces that influence the consumer include education, family, social class, ethnicity and reference groups.

INTERNAL FACTORS INFLUENCING CONSUMER CHOICE

The personal values of consumers shape all consumption decisions, but particularly of cultural products. Values can be defined as enduring beliefs on what conduct is acceptable or unacceptable. Individuals may not always act in accordance with their values, but acting in contradiction to them will often result in a state of internal unease that they will seek to avoid. Personal values, some of which the individual may be unaware, arise from the influences of family and society. From these underlying values beliefs about appropriate conduct are formed. These include whether or not to attend the arts.

Consumer Values and Beliefs

The decision to attend a cultural event may arise from the belief that a good person patronises the arts or that the arts are enjoyable. However it also may arise from a belief that cultural events are a place to gain or maintain social standing. People attending a cultural event may all say they believe in attending the arts is important, and yet each person may mean something different.

Negative beliefs about attending cultural events also exist. These beliefs must be changed by providing a positive message or a direct experience that contradicts the negative belief. However, it is true that it is difficult for cultural organisations to attract consumers who have pre-existing negative beliefs about the arts.

Of course, the influences of personal values and beliefs also combine with the individual's unique inborn personality. The interaction of all these factors results in the individual's lifestyle choices that involve the consumption of leisure, social and cultural activities.

Appeasing the Traditionalists

Some consumers' values and beliefs lead them to affirm the traditional. They do not want cultural organisations to change the way art has been presented. The New York Philharmonic Orchestra was concerned that all the emphasis on new styles of presenting concerts would turn away their traditional, conservative, older audience. So to lure them back, they held a series of traditional concerts, presented in the familiar manner along with educational events focused on increasing the audience's knowledge and appreciation of the music.

Source: Daspin, 1999.

EXTERNAL FACTORS INFLUENCING CONSUMER CHOICE

Influences from the external environment also affect motivation. These factors, which include education, family, social class, ethnicity and reference groups, shape consumer consumption decisions.

Education

Cultural organisations often consider education the most important external factor influencing the attendance decision. The common belief is that if individuals are educated about culture as children, they will feel a need to experience culture as adults. However, as stated earlier, values and beliefs, formed by family also play an equally important role in determining attendance. If these factors are negative influences, they may cancel out the positive influences of education. Even if other influences are not negative, it may not be true that exposing young people to culture at school leads to a life-time of cultural participation. Students are also exposed to math, geography and literature at school, but only a small minority continue to enjoy the subjects as adults.

However cultural organisations are correct in assuming that consumers cannot desire what they do not know. In this way, educational programmes in the schools do allow students to experience culture. The hope is that the cultural experience will be enjoyable and the student will wish to repeat it in the future (Myers, 1996).

But even if the student tries the cultural product and learns to enjoy the experience, if learning is to be retained, the experience must be repeated. One-off trips to the symphony or the art museum for groups of school children probably have little lasting effect because the children do not have the ability to repeat the experience on their own. They may attend again with their family, but in that case the family probably has already been attending cultural events.

Family

It can be debated as to whether the family or education has the largest influence on an individual's behaviour. The family certainly does play a large role in shaping the types of activities in which the family members engage. This is especially true in the area of cultural consumption. Although being raised in a culture-loving family does not automatically transform the child into a culture-consuming adult, the opposite is rarely true. The child who has grown up without the experience of being raised in a culture-loving family will rarely grow into a culture-consuming adult.

Cultural organisations might better target such educational outreach efforts to families through organisations in which they are active rather than to children through schools. After all, it is the parents who will make the attendance decision and, if they learn that the cultural experience is desirable, this will lead to increased attendance by everyone in the family.

When cultural organisations design a promotional message to motivate attendance by families, it is important to remember to target the message to both the individual who makes the consumption decision and those who will ultimately attend. When families attend a cultural event as a group, it may be the children who have heard of the event and wish to attend, but it is the parents who have made the decision. For example, the promotional message for a dinosaur exhibit would communicate to children information about fun activities, but also about its educational value to motivate the parents.

Who Attends Concerts: A Student Viewpoint

To explore their preconceptions of who attends classical concerts, as part of a research study students were asked to profile a typical classical music audience member. How did they describe the audience?

- *Older (but to the students, "older" was anyone over 35).*

- *Travels to the concert by car or taxi rather than by using public transportation.*

- *Live in nice houses in the country or suburbs, dress well, are financially well-off and are middle to upper class.*

Despite these stereotypes, the students did not have a negative bias against the audience, with only one student using the term "pompous and stuffy". They simply believed they belonged to a group with which they did not wish to associate.

Source: Kolb, 1998.

Social Class

A hierarchy of social classes exists in all societies. A social class can be defined as a group of people who associate both formally and informally and share the same value system and activities. The division on which the hierarchy is based may be wealth, birth or power, but in modern capitalistic societies, the distinction is usually based on wealth. Sociologists usually divide the class structure of these societies into high class, upper middle class, middle class, working class, working poor and underclass. This hierarchy mirrors the older distinction of social class based on birth found in more traditional societies. Social class is important as it tells us what types of cultural activities in which the members are likely to engage.

There is a historical tie between high social status and consumption of culture. Those who have been born into high positions have the time and money to pursue artistic and cultural interests. In fact, they needed some way to fill in their time, since it was not necessary to work. On the other hand, members of the middle-class often have achieved their status through hard work, which has allowed them to move up from lower classes. They now wish to associate with those from even further up the ladder of social hierarchy and may see the consumption of culture as a means of doing so. They know that the upper middle-class participate in cultural activity. By closely associating themselves with cultural organisations through attendance and by providing funding, they are emulating the behaviour of, and associating themselves with, the higher classes.

On the other hand, the working classes often do not have the time and energy to consume culture because the necessities of everyday existence take precedence. Because money is often a problem, and they have less education, their world-view is often local. As a result of this financial dependence and inward view, they do not have the same interest in attending the traditional high arts. When they do engage in cultural activities, it will more likely be a low cost, local event that they will attend with their family or other social group.

Ethnic Culture

Another external factor that affects the attendance decision is the individual's ethnic culture. Ethnic culture, the way in which members of a group approach the choices that life presents, is transmitted through life experience from one generation to the next. The decision to participate in cultural activity is not just an individual preference; it is also part of an ethnic cultural pattern.

The use of art and culture is an important component of ethnic identity. Western society's conception of culture is not universal. In the West, art is often treated as separate and sacred and is used to elevate the individual above the concerns of daily existence. Art that is used in everyday life, and enjoyed by the uneducated, is designated differently as crafts or folk art.

Many ethnic cultures have an opposite view of how art fits into society. Art in other cultures is imbedded into the social fabric of everyday life (Khan, 1996). Art will be used in rituals for important occasions such as birth, marriage and death, celebrating the recurring seasons or as objects used in everyday life, such as for working or eating. Art forms, such as music, dance and visual display, in these cultures would not be seen on an elevated level but would be viewed as part of everyday existence.

No culture consists of a totally homogeneous group; usually there is a majority culture and also one or more sub-cultures. These sub-cultures may be defined by ethnicity, but also by religion or lifestyle. The cultural organisation is often managed by individuals from the majority culture, who assume that their form of culture is universal and will be appreciated by everyone. However this is rarely the case, as art forms usually develop from the experiences of the cultural group. For this reason, art does not easily translate across cultural boundaries and may not be appreciated by someone who has not experienced the same cultural forces. All cultural groups have their own art forms that they enjoy and consider just as valid as any other.

Reaching Out to Ethnic Communities

The Cincinnati Symphony Orchestra wanted to reach out to local ethnic communities with their Classical Roots series. The method they used was partnership rather than outreach. The orchestra brought their music to three churches with predominately African-American congregations – not because they lacked music as these churches had a strong musical tradition of their own – but to share with the congregations classical music composed by African-Americans.

Source: Cincinnati Symphony, 2003.

Reference Groups

Consumer behaviour is also affected by reference groups with whom the individual chooses to associate. These groups are unrelated individuals who choose to socialise together. They include groups as diverse as amateur sports teams and gangs. Individuals will adopt the behaviour of members of the group either because they already, or wish to, belong.

The influence of reference groups is especially strong for young people because they feel a need to establish a sense of identity separate from their family. They form this identity through associating with groups that are either similar or different from their families. If they desire to be accepted by a particular group, they will need to behave in the same manner as current members. Likewise, they will avoid activities that are associated with a group with which they do not wish to be associated. Attendance at a certain type of leisure activity, such as the dance club scene, may be seen as positive because participation in the activity defines the values of those who participate or attend. Since high culture events are attended by older or conservative groups, these will be avoided.

This type of behaviour is also true of adults. If they view participating in cultural events as something that is done by a group to which they wish to belong, they will also participate. For example, if the other company employees attend opera, and they wish to be considered team players, than they will be motivated to attend opera. Likewise, if the other employees enjoy watching sports, they will likely also watch sports because of a desire to fit in with their colleagues. The challenge for cultural organisations is to package the event's ambience and style so that the activity is acceptable to the targeted group.

Price Isn't Everything or You Couldn't Pay me to Go!

At the Edinburgh Festival, the hottest ticket in town was to Wagner's Ring Cycle. Tickets normally go for hundreds of pounds so it seemed like a great idea to offer 1,900 free seats to people under 27 for Gotterdammerung.

What happened? Only 237 young people showed up for the offer and half of them left after the first interval.

Source: Holden, 2003.

In summary, consumers are motivated to purchase products that provide needed benefits. Besides the traditional benefit of experiencing the quality of the art, other benefits of arts attendance is the need to fill leisure time with a social experience and for self-improvement. Before a marketing strategy to encourage attendance can be planned, it is necessary to understand the benefits that will motivate a particular consumer group to attend the organisation's art event.

Buyer Motivation Worksheet

Besides the opportunity to experience, what else do you believe motivates your customers to attend? Use this worksheet to think of as many motivating factors as you can.

Motivation	Yes/No	Describe the Motivation in Detail
Current promotion campaign (ads, direct mail, PR, incentives)		
Personal reasons (curiosity, status, loneliness, link with organisation)		
Price (regular, special offers, season tickets)		
Location (convenience, parking, safety)		
Venue (beauty, design, historical, new)		
Family/friends (brought as part of group, dating, recommendations)		
Pleasure (physical, sensual, fun, humour, social)		
Self-improvement (lecture, programme notes, video)		

References

Blake, A. (1997) *The Land Without Music: Music, Culture and Society in Twentieth Century Britain*, Manchester University Press.

Bouder-Pailler, D. (1999) "A Model for Measuring the Goals of Theatre Attendance" in *International Journal of Arts Management*, Winter.

Bruxner, M. (1940) *Letters to a Musical Boy*, Oxford University Press.

Cincinnati Symphony (2003) online at www.cincinnatisymphony.org/news/ClassicalRoots2003.

Daspin, E. (1999) "Sex, Drugs and … Opera" in *Arts Reach*, February.

Holden, A. (2003) "Gotterdammerung? Gosh, is that the Time?: Wagner and the under-27's Fail to Click" in The Observer, August 17.

Khan, N. (1996) *The Social Impact of Arts Programme: The Tent that Covered the World*, Comedia.

Kolb, B. (1998) "Acquiring the Habit: Why People Start to Attend Classical Music Concerts: The Philharmonia Orchestra Survey Report", Unpublished paper, January.

Lahti Symphony Orchestra online at www.lahti.fi/symphony/eng/orkesteri.

Larson, G.O. (1996) *American Canvas: An Arts Legacy for Our Communities*, National Endowment for the Arts.

Maslow, A. (1987) *Motivation and Personality*, Harper & Row.

Morris, J., Degenhardt, O. and Spreadbury, H. (1998) "Brand New Awareness", in *International Arts Manager*, May.

Rosen, E. *The Anatomy of Buzz: How To Create Word of Mouth Marketing*, Doubleday, Currency.

Small, C. (1987) *Lost in Music: Culture Style and the Musical Event*, Routledge.

Small, C. (1996) *Music, Society, Education*, Wesleyan University Press.

Toronto Symphony Orchestra (2003) "It's a Party for Single Ticket Buyers on August 28 at Roy Thomson Hall" online at www.tso.on.ca/season/about/press_releases August 20.

Walsh, M. (1989) *Who's Afraid of Classical Music?*, Fireside.

Woodmansee, M. (1994) *The Author, Art, and the Market: Rereading the History of Aesthetics*, Columbia University Press.

Chapter Six

MARKET SEGMENTATION

Few cultural organisations have an audience that consists of the broadly-based spectrum of society that is the goal of their mission statements. Due to social, cultural and psychological factors, the current audience for culture is skewed toward those from the upper social class with high incomes, who are older and well educated. Because the typical arts audience represents only a segment of society, the cultural organisation needs to understand how to use segmentation to both increase and broaden its audience.

There are many methods of segmentation. One of the basic methods that can be useful for cultural organisations is to segment their audience into groups differentiated by demographic differences, such as age, marital status, income or ethnic background. In addition, they can use geographic segmentation, based on where the audience member lives. Demographic and geographic segmentation are easily understood. Segmentation by benefits, where the audience is grouped by the benefits they desire from the product is more difficult but very important to understand. Cultural organisations can also use level of involvement as a segmentation strategy and target cultural consumers and enthusiasts separately. Of course, all four methods can be used in combination, with one of the segments – demographic, geographic, benefit and involvement – used as a primary means of segmentation and then the resulting group broken down further by a secondary method of segmentation.

Concentrated *versus* Multiple Segment Targeting

Cultural organisations often use an undifferentiated targeting strategy where the entire public is treated as one large consumer market segment. In doing so, they have assumed that everyone has the same need for culture and also seeks the same benefits. However, a more successful option is concentrated targeting. With this strategy, after careful analysis of the product and its potential consumers, the cultural organisation selects a group of consumers, or segment, who will be most motivated to consume what the organisation has to offer. Since most cultural organisations have limited funds, concentrated targeting helps them to market more effectively by targeting specific segments.

By concentrating on a specific market segment, the cultural organisation can also better ensure that it can provide a product that meets the needs of the segment. It is especially true that small cultural organisations cannot be all things to all people. If small organisations focus on the needs of a specific market segment, such as families or an ethnic group, they are able to provide the services and benefits most desired by that segment. This strategy allows smaller organisations to compete more effectively with larger organisations. The promotional message of the small cultural organisation may not be heard if broadcast generally, but will be heard if targeted carefully.

Large cultural organisations may adopt a multiple segmentation strategy and target more than a single market segment. This can be done by repackaging the same cultural product for different market segments. A change in presentation style, ambience or services may be all that is necessary. For example, a concert may be offered as a matinee for families, with additional entertainment in the lobby and refreshments that appeal to young appetites. The same concert may be offered in the evening with a different ambience, using champagne and a pre-concert lecture. Likewise, the same cultural product could be offered at a different time, or even location, in order to attract a different market segment.

Another approach when targeting to multiple segments is to keep all aspects of the product the same, but to vary the message that is sent to the consumer. Even cultural organisations that do not wish to change their product can use this approach. Because cultural products provide a variety of benefits, the organisation can communicate different marketing messages that promote the benefit sought by each target market segment.

Cultural organisations should be aware that, if they choose to market to specific segments, they must continually reassess the marketplace to ensure that their choice is still correct. With today's fast pace of demographic and social change, the benefits desired by market segments can change quickly.

Developing a New Market Segment

The aim of Asian Arts Access, based in the UK, is both to promote the creation of art and to create a market for the art product. It works to promote South Asian arts in the UK for both Asian and cross-cultural audiences. It focuses on collaborative projects, aimed at both creative development and building a market segment for Asian art.

Source: Asian Art, 2004.

AUDIENCE SEGMENTATION STRATEGY

The development of both the size and range of the audience is the central responsibility of the marketing department. It is responsible for increasing the size of the audience, but this would also be true of the marketing department of any commercial business, since more customers results in more revenue.

However, audience development in a cultural organisation also means increasing the range of the audience. Commercial businesses will also wish to increase the range, but only as a means to increase the size of the customer base so as to increase revenue for the company. Because reaching a broad range of people with their art is the central mission of cultural organisations, they view increasing the range of the audience as a goal in itself. Indeed, they will spend considerable resources to reach and attract non-attending groups, even when the customers bring in limited additional revenue. The goal of the cultural organisation is to expose as many people as possible from a broad spectrum of society to their art product. This focus on mission before money is a fundamental difference between them and a for-profit company.

Market Depth

As a first step in the process of segmentation of their current and potential audience, cultural organisations must decide whether to develop market depth, breadth or both. To develop market depth, the cultural organisation first must determine its current audience segment and then develop a marketing strategy that attracts more members of this same group. This has been the traditional strategy of cultural organisations. It is an easy strategy, because the cultural organisation is already familiar with its current audience and what motivates them to attend. However following this approach will result in limited growth in attendance, as most people in this segment are already aware of the organisation and have made their decision on whether to attend.

City Opera in New York: Something for Everyone

City Opera knows that opera lovers vary. So the programming it provides varies also, with different programming targeted at different groups. The City Opera audience can be divided into:

Audience Segment	*Cultural Product*
People new to opera	*Standard repertoire*
Well-informed opera fans	*New opera repertoire*
Culturally curious cross-overs	*Opera combined with theatre repertoire*

City Opera also seeks to differentiate itself from the New York Metropolitan Opera:

City	*Met*
Rethinking opera favourites	*Performing repertoire in the traditional manner*
Younger, emerging singers	*World-renowned singers*
Singers who look like characters	*Star names*

Source: Tommasini, 1999.

Market Breadth

If the cultural organisation wishes to expand the audience for its product by developing market breadth, its must attract members of new market segments who may be currently consuming other cultural products. In addition, because consumers have other means of using leisure time besides consuming culture, it will also need to attract consumers away from competing products, such as other forms of entertainment. To do so, cultural organisations must be willing to adjust the benefits provided by their cultural product, so that they can attract consumers in new market segments who are currently consuming other products.

The consumers in these new market segments may desire different benefits than the cultural organisation's current audience. Therefore, the cultural organisation needs to use benefit segmentation to differentiate their cultural product, so that they can market to the new segment of the population while also retaining their current audience.

SEGMENTATION PROCESS

The first step in the segmentation process is for the cultural organisation to determine what segments are in their current audience. Based on this information, it then must determine what new or potential segments it will target as audience members. The cultural organisation then must develop a promotional message that communicates effectively to each targeted segment.

Market segmentation is particularly useful for small cultural organisations. It may seem a betrayal of the organisation's mission, because it means going after a smaller targeted market segment rather than trying to attract everyone. Unfortunately, cultural organisations must face the fact that it may be an unrealistic expectation that everyone will be interested in their product. Therefore, they can not consider everyone a potential attender. Besides, small organisations do not have the resources for a large marketing effort, and market segmentation allows them to save time and effort, and perhaps even ensure survival, by concentrating their marketing resources.

DEFINING THE TARGET SEGMENT

Because there are numerous ways to segment markets, a cultural organisation may feel confused when faced with the process of segmenting its current or potential audience. Nevertheless the process of analysing and segmenting will assist the organisation in thinking through who they serve, how they serve them and who they wish to serve in the future.

In traditional marketing theory, the process of segmentation is started first by examining either consumers or the product. The company may decide first to analyse the existing consumer marketplace and then to develop a product that meets a segment's needs. Or it may start with its existing product and find a market segment that desires the product's benefits.

Cultural organisations could begin by choosing a market segment to target and then designing a product to provide the desired benefits to this segment. However, cultural organisations have usually not done this, as they have felt that they should not change their cultural product to meet the desires of the public. Cultural organisations have usually used the segmentation process to find a market segment to which their existing cultural product will appeal.

However it is possible for a cultural organisation first to target a market segment and then to design its cultural product in a manner that will appeal to this segment, without compromising its mission. For example, it may present a specialised form of its current art, which would still fall in the scope of its mission but also appeal to a new target market segment.

Whichever initial focus cultural organisations take, either product or market, they must ensure that the group targeted is distinct enough to qualify as a market segment. For example, a cultural organisation may decide to focus on providing the benefits sought by younger consumers, but this segment is too broad to be workable. The segmentation process would be more effective if the cultural organisation divided young consumers into sub-groups such as well-educated, upper-middle-class singles and less-educated, lower-middle-class parents. Also, young consumers may be from the dominant ethnic group or from a minority group. The only common characteristic the young share is age and that is not enough to target them effectively as a segment. The benefits they seek will be too diverse for the organisation to be able to meet all the needs of all young people.

METHODS OF SEGMENTATION

Every cultural organisation needs to examine its existing audience and also the audience it wishes to attract. Most cultural organisations are familiar with using demographic data to segment their audience on the basis of age, gender, income and ethnicity. While this is an important first step, the cultural organisation makes a mistake when it assumes that consumers in these segments, even though they have similar demographic characteristics, will always desire similar benefits. There are other methods that can be used to segment markets and a cultural organisation is not restricted to only segmenting its audience by a single method.

Targeting Residents in Low-income Communities

Community arts programmes are popular in all types of neighbourhoods, as they improve both the social and economic climate. This is true also for low-income neighbourhoods. In fact, residents in these areas are just as involved with local community arts organisations as residents in more affluent neighbourhoods.

But low-income residents are much less likely to be involved in their regional cultural institutions. It is in the interest of these larger cultural institutions to partner with local organisations to build a bridge to these communities and encourage the residents to become more involved on a regional, not just local, basis.

Source: Zorn, 1998/99.

Demographic Segmentation

For small cultural organisations, demographic segmentation is usually a good first step in the segmentation process. The demographic factors used can include gender, age, education level, occupation, marital status, income and ethnicity. Marketing departments for profit companies use income segmentation to determine how consumers' consumption decisions are affected by the amount of available *income*, so they can market to the appropriate income segment. Because the cultural audience is already dominated by high-income individuals, cultural organisations face a particular challenge when attempting to reach other income-level market segments. Many consumers outside of the high-income segment will have already decided that the price for attending is too high, even though this may not be the case. If the preconception exists that the performance or event will be too expensive, it is necessary for the cultural organisation to communicate strongly to lower income market segments that there are opportunities to attend events at reasonable prices.

If the only marketing message on the availability of affordable ticket prices is a small statement at the bottom of a brochure which was designed to attract the high income market segment, it will probably not be read by those who most need to receive the message. To reach those who may believe that the cost to attend is too high, the low cost must be communicated directly to this group.

Probably the greatest challenge faced by cultural organisations is the need to segment by *ethnicity* to attract a more ethnically-diverse audience. Of course, cultural organisations will insist that everyone is welcome, which is true. It is also true that for most cultural organisations, particularly those that present high culture, the audience consists of members of the majority ethnic group. To attract other ethnic segments successfully, it is not enough for the cultural organisation to use segmentation as a means to attract members of other groups to the existing culture product. It must also determine how its product can be made more attractive to a specific ethnic population segment.

Rather than just decry the lack of participation, by exploring the needs and desires of the different ethnic communities cultural organisations can take active steps to ensure that all segments of the community who are interested feel welcome to participate (Radbourne and Fraser, 1996). This may mean presenting the cultural product in a different manner or at a different location or time, since ethnic culture not only affects the choice of leisure consumption, it also affects the pattern of socialisation. For example, in Western culture, many cultural events are considered "adults-only", which will negatively affect the attendance rate for a cultural group where family interaction is highly valued. Members of these cultural groups will prefer cultural events that are planned for the family to attend together.

Another issue for particular ethnic groups is that cultural organisations may be seen as presenting the art of the majority, and perhaps oppressive, ethnic group. Ethnic minority groups may not be interested in applauding art that seems to negate them as individuals. It is important for cultural organisations to ensure that their cultural product is also created, and presented, by individuals other than members of the majority culture.

Geographic Segmentation

Geographic segmentation is also an easy way to segment. It is important for the organisation to determine how far most consumers are travelling to attend their venue, so they will know where and what media to use in promotion. Small cultural organisations may depend on *local* audiences and find it impossible to attract consumers to come from a distance, when there are other cultural organisations that provide the consumer with the same benefits. However if the cultural product offered is unique and attractive to a specific segment of the market, then carefully targeted communication can bring customers from *outside* the local area.

On the other hand, if the cultural organisation is large and well-known, geographic barriers may not exist. In fact, the cultural product may be the reason why individuals are travelling to the area. "Superstar" organisations such as the British Museum and the Metropolitan Opera in New York have local visitors but also attract many international *tourists* for which they are a "must-see" during their visit (Murphy, 1997).

A Student's Profile of the Current Classical Music Market Segment

When students were asked who attends classical music concerts, they all believed the audience had access to some special knowledge that others do not have. They described the audience as "very musical types of people" who "have studied and appreciate music" and as "intellectuals with cultural backgrounds". Students who were from a minority ethnic group described the audience as "white" and "European".

There was general agreement among the students that, to attend classical music concerts, it was necessary to first acquire this special knowledge. Or as one student explained, "If you don't know about it, you might enjoy music that is bad, that educated people would know was bad, and then you'd feel stupid". As they explained, with pop music you either like a song or do not like it, but that's not considered to be right or wrong. Therefore, they stated they would not feel at ease at a concert, because they would not have done the prerequisite self-education and improvement necessary to understand the music. The traditional concert audience has become associated in the minds of the students as educated and elitist and therefore people with whom they would not be comfortable associating.

Source: Kolb, 1998.

Benefit Segmentation

While demographic and geographic segmentation are good first steps in analysing the audience for culture, benefit segmentation, which focuses on the different benefits that are desired as a result of such factors as lifestyles, usage rate and motivation, is a more powerful segmentation tool for cultural organisations. When analysing the current and potential audience, desired benefits may not be as easily discernible as demographic or geographic factors, but they are the factors that actually motivate the consumer to attend a cultural event.

Benefit segmentation attempts to understand and group consumers based on the characteristics of how they spend their time, what they purchase and their psychographic characteristics. For example, a cultural organisation may find that their audience divides into *lifestyle* segments, consisting of the young and trendy and the older and conservative. The benefits sought by members of these segments will vary but are closely related to their lifestyle. The benefits could be as dissimilar as an opportunity to socialise with friends, family time together, and a comforting, familiar cultural experience.

The cultural organisation also needs to determine how frequently each segment group consumes their product. The young and trendy may be occasional attenders for some art forms, such as symphonic concerts, and yet may be heavy consumers of modern dance. The *usage* pattern of the old and sedate may be just the opposite. Young family groups may be heavy users of museums that allow their children to participate in activities but not serious drama. Once the cultural organisation is aware of the attendance frequency, it can decide upon the resources, it should devote to marketing to each target market segment.

Most cultural organisations do not have *psychographic* information on their audiences because it is difficult to obtain and analyse. It is true that these market segments are not immediately apparent, and focus groups and interviews will need to be conducted to discover the benefits that motivate the various groups to attend. But once this information is obtained, and it is correlated with demographic and geographic factors, it can be used to design a very effective strategy to target the resulting market segments.

Reality as a Benefit

In an increasingly cyber and wired world, arts can offer the benefit of reality. It is predicted by Pamela Danziger, a market researcher, that there will be a return of interest in the 'real' world.

"As our world goes more cyber, consumers will feel the need to surround themselves with things that will bring them back to reality."

This is a message that cultural organisations can use to target those burned out by a cyber world. After all what is more real than a live performance experience?

Source: Danziger, 2002.

Level of Involvement Segmentation

Developing a market segmentation strategy is easier for large organisations with the resources to differentiate their product by packaging cultural events. For example, a museum may offer family activities (demographic), hotel packages that include tickets for visitors to the area (geographic) and "singles" nights (benefit) all for the same exhibit.

This approach is more difficult for smaller cultural organisations that may need to use all their resources in producing one type of product. The target marketing strategy usually favoured by such organisations is to target the segment that already desires the benefits provided by their product.

The small cultural organisation can increase the attendance of its audience by segmenting them according to their level of involvement with the art form. Attendance by cultural enthusiasts can be maintained by providing them the opportunities for learning and involvement, while attendance of culture consumers can be increased by providing them with entertainment.

Reaching the Youth Segment Using Verdi

There is a lot of talk about making art socially relevant for young people. And yet what can be more relevant than love and heartbreak? You just need to let them know that's what La Traviata is about. Their reaction?

> *"Some were still dabbing away tears at the tragic death of Violetta; as well as discovering that posh music can be moving, they had received a stern lesson in love. Few Yorkshire fathers, perhaps, would these days persuade their son's girlfriend to break his heart by leaving him, lest her murky past damage his sister's future; but the very human tragedy that is Verdi's masterpiece remains undimmed by time."*

Source: Holden, 2003.

CAPITALISING ON SEGMENTATION

Cultural organisations tend to be insular, perhaps because people working in cultural organisations share a similar vision that is not constrained by the everyday reality in which most people live. Because of this insularity, there is a danger that the organisation will become so focused on the importance of its cultural product that it will forget that the product is not a priority for most people. Because the cultural organisation believes that everyone *should be* interested in its product, it can come to believe that everyone *is* interested in its product. The result is that the cultural organisation tries to communicate everything to everyone, rather than to communicate a specific message to a specific group.

The cultural organisation might broadcast the same marketing message to everyone as if there is only one unsegmented market. Or, it might consider each individual entirely unique, which makes it extremely difficult to design a marketing message. Both methods are ineffective, as while all individuals do differ, they also share some similar characteristics. By focusing on these similar characteristics, the cultural organisation can improve the chance of attracting the consumer to the product.

The cultural organisation can communicate much more effectively if it channels each communication about its product to a specific market segment. The members of the group may, or may not, share similar demographic characteristics. What is similar is that those belonging to the segment all feel a shared need for the specific benefits the cultural product offers. Once an organisation has determined the market segment it wishes to target, it can design a marketing message that communicates directly to this segment.

However after segmenting the audience using one or more of these factors, the cultural organisation often makes the mistake of only using this information to modify its marketing message. It may change the type, layout and copy of a brochure or the media in which it advertises so that it will be more attractive to a new market segment. While this is a valid approach, market segmentation is most useful on a more basic level by finding the correct match between the cultural product and the audience.

"Those Exotic Europeans and Their Curious Ways"

New York City, of which Brooklyn is a part, was 91% white (or of European heritage) in 1950. In the year 2000, according to the US census, it was only 35% white. So that means that the white population is no longer the ethnic majority in the City. The Brooklyn Museum of Art has many fine exhibit halls once called 'ethnic' including Egyptian, African, Meso-American. They have now opened a European hall. As a review of the museum points out:

> *"In reality, of course, European painting is ethnic art, with all the exoticism, inscrutability and 'otherness' that implies. Far from representing a universal aesthetic gold standard, it is the product of specific times and places, beliefs and taboos."*

Source: Cotter, 2003.

Message Focus

When everyone is constantly bombarded with advertising, it makes sense for the cultural organisation to focus only on communicating to the specific target market that will be most attracted to their product. Once the cultural organisation has determined the benefits desired from its product by each target segment, it can then determine a communication style attractive to the segment. The cultural organisation may be able to attract young people to an event using an exciting brochure and message. But if the young people who attend desire an opportunity to socialise as a benefit of attendance, and do not find the benefit they desire, they will learn to mistrust the messages from the organisation and will not return.

Cultural organisations have been using target marketing for their current audience. However, in the current competitive environment, cultural organisations that wish to increase attendance must design marketing strategies for each specific market segment they wish to target. Even in profit companies, the days of mass marketing are gone. Now, rather than have a single strategy and try to attract everyone, the organisation must develop a targeted marketing strategy focused on a particular group.

Arts marketing has been traditionally described as the process of finding an audience for the art. A better description of arts marketing would be the process of determining what segment of the population can be interested in the product and then determining how to motivate them to attend by providing appropriately packaged arts events.

To do this successfully, the responsibilities of arts marketing should be expanded to include the process of segmenting the current and potential audience, using research to determine the needs and desires of these segments and designing a promotional strategy to motivate them to attend. This cannot be done without the co-operation of the rest of the organisation, including the artistic department, because the entire organisation must contribute to designing the packaged product.

TOURISTS AS A MARKET SEGMENT

Growth in travel opportunities and improved communication systems has contributed to an increased awareness of global culture. Consumers are now familiar with the art and music of many other countries besides their own. It is natural that they would want to visit cultural organisations to experience these art forms when they travel. Heritage sites and museums, along with theatres and other performing arts venues, are a significant reason why tourists visit the major urban areas (Hughes, 1997).

As government funding provided to cultural organisations for operational expenses has decreased, cultural organisations have become increasingly interested in attracting cultural tourists to their venues. Targeting cultural tourists is a means for cultural organisations to earn additional revenue, while still being true to their mission.

Rationale for Targeting Tourists

Besides offering an opportunity to increase its audience, a cultural organisation should market to tourists for the same reasons it would wish to market to anyone – to expose others to its art form. In addition, by marketing to the cultural tourist, it provides visitors with a cultural opportunity unavailable to them at home.

What Exactly is Cultural Tourism?

There are many definitions, so perhaps an example would be better. The state of Victoria in Australia has put together an arts, theatre and cultural heritage plan for 2002–2006. It defines the experiences that cultural tourists might engage in as:

- *Visiting historic sites to learn about the Australian Gold Rush*
- *Being part of community festivals*
- *Enjoying Victoria's rich multicultural offerings*
- *Visiting artists working in their studios and galleries*
- *Attending a theatre performance*
- *Enjoying steam travel via train and paddle boat experiences.*

Source: Tourism Victoria, 2004.

Ideally, the tourist is travelling to gain an understanding of foreign countries and cultures but, in reality, most tourists are travelling for enjoyment. Therefore, cultural tourists want an experience that is both exciting and memorable, so that they can share the experience with friends and family when they return home. Even so cultural tourists are also interested in education programmes – as long as they are enjoyable – that will help them understand what they are experiencing. Because tourists often have a crowded itinerary, they will have limited time to spend at each place they visit. The cultural organisation faces the additional challenge of providing a worthwhile experience for the tourist in a very short time period.

Tourists often visit cultural organisations out of a feeling of obligation. They know that there are certain sites that they must see on their trip, so they visit the historic sites, museums and performances that are listed in their guidebook or that their friends or relatives visited on their holidays. When in London, they must visit the British Museum and, when in Paris, they must visit the Louvre. Cultural tourists feel a need to visit these cultural organisations, because it is part of the expected holiday experience. But if the cultural organisation can successfully expose these tourists to new cultural experiences, they will also bring home a new knowledge of culture.

Issues in Targeting Tourists

While the idea of having access to an additional target market interested in their art form may be attractive to cultural organisations, the organisation must consider carefully whether to promote to tourists (Boniface, 1995). If the cultural organisation feels that the potential tourist market segment desires benefits that conflict too dramatically with the organisation's mission, it might not wish to market to tourists. For example, if the cultural organisation's primary goal is to educate visitors on a rather obscure and difficult art form, while the tourist's primary goal is enjoying the sun and surf, it may be too difficult to create an experience that is satisfactory to the tourist while also meeting the mission of the organisation.

Another reason for not promoting to the tourist market is where the cultural experience is too specific to the country where the cultural organisation is located. In this case, it may not be understandable or attractive to tourists because it is too culturally distinctive. And a third negative consideration is that, in meeting the needs of tourists, the organisation may not be able to meet its responsibilities to the established local market segments it already serves.

Reasons for Not Promoting to Tourists

- Conflicting goals.
- Art form too culturally distinctive to be attractive to tourists.
- Alienate current audience.

WHO ARE CULTURAL TOURISTS?

Of course, "tourists" is too broad a category to target easily. The tourist market needs to be further segmented into the demographic and psychographic groups that are most likely to be attracted to cultural activities.

Segments of the tourist market that are attracted to culture include *older* visitors. These older tourists are naturally inclined toward culture, because of their socialisation experiences and they probably also patronise cultural organisations when they are at home. Another group interested in cultural organisations, but for a different reason, are *younger* tourists. They may consider attending a cultural event while travelling in another country as an adventure. But they may not attend the same event at home, where it would be considered less exciting. For this reason, cultural tourism is an excellent means of exposing young people to cultural experiences in which they might not otherwise participate.

The tourist market can also be further segmented by the benefits sought by the tourists (Boniface, 1995). Some cultural tourists seek *escapism*. They want an experience that is different from those they experience in daily life. Other tourists want their visit to a cultural organisation to provide them with a feeling of *status*. They want a unique experience unobtainable elsewhere, of which they can boast when they have returned home.

There are also smaller target markets of speciality cultural tourists. Some speciality cultural tourists travel with the purpose of meeting *religious* or *spiritual* needs. They want to connect with their values by visiting sites, which may be as varied as Westminster Abbey and Stonehenge. Other speciality cultural tourists travel with the specific purpose of doing *research* or receiving education. For these tourists, who are often students, professionals or hobbyists, knowledge is the most important benefit derived from cultural tourism.

Target Segments of the Tourist Market

- Escapists.
- Status-seekers.
- Religionists and spiritualists.
- Researchers and students.

Global Culture is Nothing New

"We are increasingly aware that culture undergoes a constant process of global circulation and that it had done so long before the advent of international telecommunications or the emergence of the so-called international art market. When we look at the histories of fashion, textiles, and decoration, of food and drink, of colours and shades, of poetic expression, of the sexual imagination, we understand that from the beginning of mobility there had always been a circulation and a cross-cultural translation and that we simply did not have the means and awareness by which to narrate this process."

Source: Rogoff, 1998.

Needs of the Tourist Segment

Some of the benefits desired by tourists visiting a cultural organisation may be similar to the benefits desired by other visitors, but cultural tourists do have some additional needs for which the cultural organisation must provide. Because cultural tourists are unfamiliar with the country's culture, and not just the cultural product, they need to be provided with even more *information* about the history and meaning of the art form. Cultural tourists will not bring the same assumptions and knowledge as the local residents and need additional information so that they can understand and enjoy what they see.

Because they are visitors, cultural organisations should ensure that tourists are especially made to feel *welcome* when visiting the venue. The tourist market gives cultural organisations an excellent means to attract people to a new experience that they may feel uncomfortable with at home. The tourist might not visit a cultural organisation at home because they feel they don't belong, but while travelling, they may be ready to take the risk.

Tourists who are travelling a long distance to visit the cultural organisation have a need for the experience to be as they expected it to be. The cultural organisation must provide a certain amount of *dependability* in the cultural product presented to tourists. The experience needs to be consistent over time so that tourists will have a similar experience to that of their friends, who may have visited last year. This does not mean that the product must be absolutely the same, but that it needs to be of the type expected.

Because the cultural tourist is unfamiliar with the local area, it is also very important that all marketing and media messages contain sufficient information on *location*, including information on how to travel to the site using public transportation. If the organisation is located in an out-of-the-way area, cultural tourists also need to be provided with information that addresses any safety concerns they may have. And, because they are tourists and want to have *fun*, they need information on opportunities for shopping and eating.

Needs of Cultural Tourists

- Additional information on the cultural product.
- Welcoming environment.
- Dependable product.
- Location information.
- Opportunity for amusement.

CULTURAL TOURISM & THE COMMUNITY

The wider community increasingly sees cultural organisations that serve tourists as a source of revenue and employment (Broadway, 1997). Government agencies have become aware of the positive effect cultural tourism has on economic growth and are starting to collaborate with cultural and tourism groups to promote such tourism. In fact, besides promotion of the art itself, one of the main rationales for having music festivals or major exhibitions is to attract tourists to visit an area.

Because of the generation of employment and income for profit businesses used by tourists, cultural tourism may also be supported by the businesses in the community in which the organisation is located. Cultural tourism can help the entire community through regeneration of an economically-depressed area and, as a result, increase the status of the community. If cultural organisations work together in attracting cultural tourists, they will be seen by others as an integral part of the community.

In summary, segmentation is a tool cultural organisations can use to better understand their current audience. They can then use segmentation to determine which groups of people might be most interested in their product. This does not mean they are uninterested in having others attend. However the reality is that most small cultural organisations must use their limited resources wisely. By carefully targeting a market segment, they are more likely to be able to successfully motivate attendance.

Segmentation Worksheet

Describe your most typical audience member using segmentation. Then describe a new audience segment you would like to also have in your audience.

Variable	Our Current Audience Segment	Our New Target Segment
Demographic: (What is their age, gender, income, occupation, race/ethnic, social class and family stage?)		
Geographic: (Are they from the neighbourhood, city, region or tourists?)		
Benefit: (Did they come for opportunity to learn, to socialise, to be excited, to gain status, find a date or for a family activity?)		
Level of Involvement: (Did they come for entertainment, to learn more about art, or to socialise with others with similar interests?)		

Now answer these questions on how your typical audience member uses your product. The more 'yes' answers, the higher the level of involvement with your organisation. It is important to keep them attending even while you attract a new audience. The fewer 'yes' answers the more important it is market to new consumer segments.

Usage questions	Yes	No	?
Do they attend frequently?			
Are they a member of your organisation?			
Do they volunteer?			
Do they provide additional financial support?			
Are they loyal to your organisation vs. competition?			
Are they interested in new products or only one type?			
Are the numbers in this group increasing?			

References

Asian Arts Access (2004) online at www.asianartsaccess.org.

Boniface, P. (1995) *Managing Quality Cultural Tourism*, Routledge.

Broadway, M.J. (1997) "Urban Tourism Development in the Modern Canadian City: A Review" in *Quality Management in Urban Tourism*, Wiley. Hughes, H.L. (1997) "Urban Tourism and the Performing Arts" in *Quality Management in Urban Tourism*, Wiley.

Cotter, H. (2003) "Those Exotic Europeans and Their Curious Ways" in *New York Times*, October 3.

Danziger, P. (2002) *Why People Buy Things They Don't Need*, Paramount Market Publishing.

Holden, Anthony (2003) "We Second That Emotion: Twentysomethings are turning to opera for a great night out" in *The Observor* Oct 12, 2003.

Hughes, H.L. (1997) "Urban Tourism and the Performing Arts" in *Quality Management in Urban Tourism*, Wiley.

Kolb, B. (1998) "Acquiring the Habit: Why People Start to Attend Classical Music Concerts: The Philharmonia Orchestra Survey Report", Unpublished paper, January.

Murphy, P.E. (1997) *Quality Management in Urban Tourism*, John Wiley & Sons.

Radbourne, J. and Fraser, M. (1996) *Arts Management: A Practical Guide*, Allen and Unwin.

Rogoff, I. (1998) "Twenty Years On ... Inside, Out" in *Art Journal*, December 22.

Tommasini, A. (1999) "A New Season, a New Sound" in *New York Times*, September 10.

Tourism Victoria (2004) "Victoria's Arts, Theatre and Cultural Heritage Plan 2002–2006" online at www.tourismvictoria.com.au/arts/plan.

Zorn, J. (1998/99) "The Benefits of Neighbourhood Culture" in *Arts Reach*, December/January.

Chapter Seven

USING RESEARCH

The marketing concept states that the cultural organisation must listen to the wants and needs of the consumer. The only means to discover these wants and needs is through conducting research. This requires knowledge of the types and purposes of research, the research process, classifications of research and research methods.

Most cultural organisations already conduct research to find who and how many are attending by "counting bums on seats". Unfortunately, they are less likely to conduct research on why their audience attends and what benefits they are seeking. This may be because managers of cultural organisations often assume that the audience is motivated by the same reason they attend themselves. This is highly unlikely, since individuals who work in cultural organisations have an enthusiasm for the art form that goes far beyond what most other people feel. Because of this enthusiasm, the cultural organisation may object to conducting marketing research because it believes it knows already what its audience wants and sees research as a waste of money.

In reality, it is vital for the cultural organisation to know what motivates its audience to attend. Research does not need to be expensive, but it does take effort. First the organisation needs to understand the types and methods of research. It needs to learn the research process and the use of the different research tools. With this knowledge, research can be used successfully even by small cultural organisations on limited budgets.

TYPES OF RESEARCH

Besides basic audience research that tells the organisation who is attending, there are other types of research a cultural organisation should consider conducting. Competitor research is rarely conducted but can provide valuable information on how an organisation can improve. Cultural organisations should analyse their audience's perception of competitors and also visit the competitors themselves. Such research helps the organisation to determine whether it should attempt to add any of the services, programmes or amenities provided by organisations producing competing products.

Motivation research examines the consumers' reasons for attendance and is critical to increasing and broadening the audience. Satisfaction research is conducted after the art product has been consumed to examine how the experience compares with customer expectations. Information gathered from both motivational and satisfaction research will help the cultural organisation to learn whether and how they need to improve. The organisation also needs to focus internally, by routinely examining the product it offers to determine whether it can be improved.

Types and Purpose of Research

Types	Purpose	Research Question
Audience	Composition of current audience	Who is in our audience?
Competitor	Audience perception of competition	Where else do they attend and why?
Motivation	Reasons for attendance	Why do they attend?
Satisfaction	Extent event meets expectations	Are we doing anything wrong?
Product	Improvement of product	Does our product provide the desired benefits?
Promotional	Effectiveness of different messages and media	Where and how do they hear about us?
Pricing	Choosing pricing levels	What do they think of our price?
Policy	Attitudes toward the arts	Who out there supports us?

Another type of research that is vital is promotional research. This research seeks to determine whether the message the cultural organisation is communicating is reaching its target audience and whether the message is effectively motivating attendance by communicating the desired benefits. Pricing research is conducted to determine whether the audience perceives the price as appropriate and competitive

Because cultural organisations are dependent on government funders for support, they are vulnerable to changes in government policies in the level of their support for the arts. But since many cultural organisations are also now dependent on corporate support, they need to be aware of changes in patterns of corporate giving as well. For these reasons, cultural organisations need to conduct policy research to keep abreast of attitudes toward supporting culture.

You Call This Fun?

Little research has been done on what benefits young people derive from the experience of attending a classical concert. The purpose of this inexpensive study was to learn the benefits that would motivate young people to attend classical music concerts. Groups of students who had never attended a classical concert were taken to a concert using donated tickets. A focus group was used before and after the concert to explore their opinions and reactions.

Each group of five to seven students attended a different type of concert, including a traditional concert with music by Wagner, Dvorák and Sibelius, a "pops" classical concert and a concert featuring new compositions by Michael Nyman.

Focus groups held prior to attending the concert concentrated on determining the students' preconceptions of classical music, classical music patrons and the experience of attending a concert. After the concert, the students were asked what they liked best and least about the concert and how they felt the concert experience could be improved. The focus groups were planned to be as informal as possible. Besides open-ended questions and discussion, projective techniques were used to obtain information, including asking the students to write advertisements for a classical music concert and asking them to complete cartoons of the typical classical music patron.

The results? They liked the music but recommended:

- *More comfortable seats*
- *Better food choices*
- *Free programmes*
- *More visual stimulation in the hall*
- *Friendly-looking musicians*

Source: Kolb, 1999.

CONDUCTING MARKETING RESEARCH

Too often, the research done by cultural organisations is conducted without proper planning. The research process consists of six steps.

The Research Process

1. Designing the research question
What do we want to know?

↓

2. Deciding on the source of information
Who has the information we need?

↓

3. Choosing the research method
Which type and method will we use?

↓

4. Creating the research design
Where, when and how will the research be done?

↓

5. Conducting the research
Just go do it!

↓

6. Analysing and reporting the findings
What does it mean?

Only after the first step, designing the research question, should the organisation proceed with its research. Because cultural organisations are often in a hurry for answers, the temptation is to start the research before determining what they really want to know. As a result, they may ask too many questions and try to obtain too much information from too many sources. To be effective, a research study must be both well-designed and narrowly-focused. If the research question is too broad, too much information will be obtained. The mass of resulting data will be difficult to analyse and, therefore, of little use to the organisation. Even worse, if the wrong question is asked, the research effort will be wasted.

Likewise, the cultural organisation needs to put considerable thought into determining the sources from which the information can be obtained. The different sources for data are categorised as secondary or desk – data that already exists – and primary data that the organisation collects itself.

What Do You Look Like to a Stranger?

Here is what the experience of a visit to the Kirov Ballet at Covent Garden is like to someone who has never been there before because she usually attends rock concerts:

> *"The Opera House itself, meanwhile, is a sumptuous edifice. And it should be, given the quite unbelievable generosity of thousands of ordinary Lottery players who wouldn't normally go to the opera or the ballet – the Great Untutu-ed (I include myself). It all makes a very pleasant change, however, from the squalid basements ankle-deep in drink and worse where rock is played.*
>
> *There are millions of ladies toilets too. This is because there are millions of ladies. Perhaps the Saturday matinee audience weights the male-female ratio, unduly, but going to the ballet seems akin to going to the changing rooms of a department store: the men trail stoically in the wake of great gangs of chirruping women. All my previous experience of audiences suggests that vast swathes of humans shout and smell like spilled beer. Here, there's a faint miasma of rose petal. Can they smell my fear?*
>
> *I'm on my own, but happily, there are free copies of the* Financial Times *available in the foyer to hide in. Free things are always good – the kind of people the Opera House wants to attract nowadays really like free things. But free FTs are evidence of this august institution's dilemma; trying to convince ordinary folk the Opera isn't all that posh, while convincing the posh that it is."*

Source: Empire, 2003.

Desk Research

Desk research should be conducted first to find any already existing sources of information. Sources of secondary data include internal data that the organisation already possesses, perhaps in a customer database. Even just analysing existing sales data can be helpful in discovering events and days or times that attract a larger audience than others.

Other sources of information include previously conducted and published surveys that can be obtained through the government, arts council offices or public libraries. Much of this information can now be obtained online. If there are sufficient funds available, information can be purchased from commercial research firms whose business is to gather data.

EUCLID in Europe, and CPANDA in the US, maintain databases of existing government and cultural organisation research. It may be that the question that needs to be answered has already been asked. This is particularly true for policy issues. Data on attendance demographics for art forms is also readily available. Even if the information is not specific to the organisation, it can be used as a comparison.

Why Qualitative Techniques and Not Just a Quantitative Survey?

As qualitative researcher Shay Sayre states:

> *"We're not opposed to statistics, math, or counting. We just use them as starting points or to strengthen our findings. We incorporate, combine, and integrate data-gathering methods for an in-depth understanding of our research question."*

Source: Sayre, 2001.

Primary Research

Primary research involves the generation and collection of quantitative and/or qualitative data from individuals, usually through surveys, interviews or in focus groups. In addition there are others methods of collecting primary data besides directly asking consumers. Simply observing the audience to see whether, and how, they are enjoying the product and any difficulties they may be having while at the venue can provide considerable data that will help the organisation to improve both its product and service. Indeed, if the organisation wishes to change the product or service in an effort to improve the benefits, it may wish to experiment first by trying the change on a small scale and observing the effect it has on consumers.

The next step is to choose a research method. Understanding how the cultural organisation plans to use the information will help it to design the study appropriately. If the organisation wishes to impress a government office with the number and diversity of its audience, then a simple demographic survey would be appropriate. If, on the other hand, the organisation wishes to discover why attendance is falling, it will need in-depth information that cannot be obtained through a simple survey, but will require focus groups or interviews.

After choosing the research method, the cultural organisation must plan the research design. This will include the details of when the research will be conducted, where and by whom. The more planning of the details that is done, the more smoothly the research will proceed. The planning should include all details. Everything, from how many copies of the survey form are needed to who will be responsible for ensuring that the focus group participants arrive, should be considered.

Finally, the cultural organisation is ready to conduct the research. Once done, the final task is analysing the data and reporting the results. Analysing requires repeatedly going over and over the collected responses to see common themes, patterns and connections.

Question: What are a CPANDA and a EUCLID?

Possible answers: *a) small furry animals*
                        b) databases

If you guessed the second answer, you are correct! CPANDA, is a new interactive digital archive of data on US arts and cultural policy on which you will find data on artists, arts and cultural organisations, audiences and funding.

It can answer questions such as:

> *How many people participate in arts and cultural activities?*
>
> *How do people find out about arts events in their communities?*
>
> *Do places of worship make good arts venues?*
>
> *What about public libraries?*

EUCLID has been around longer and has a database called ACRONIM that contains thousands of entries on cultural research, including reports, conference papers and post-graduate theses. The database is searchable by theme, geographic area and key words. And it's free!

Don't start your research from scratch when there is so much information already available!

Source: CPANDA (2004) and EUCLID (2004).

THE RESEARCH QUESTION

It may seem easy at first, but deciding exactly what you want to know can be difficult and time-consuming. However, unless this question is answered correctly, the rest of the research might be a wasted effort. When designing the research question, the following issues should be kept in mind:

- What is our objective for this research?
- Where and how can the information be obtained?
- How do we plan to use the findings?

The first question most cultural organisations want answered is "who are our current audience members". They may also want to know why they come and where else they attend. The answers to these questions tell the organisation what benefits motivate their current audience. They also tell them what competitors are attracting their audience, so they can assess the benefits their competitors provide.

While these questions are certainly valid and important information, they do not tell the cultural organisation how to attract new groups of consumers who are not attending. Therefore, the organisation also needs to research the question of what would bring in new consumers who do not attend and also, if possible, how to attract customers of its competitors. Because these consumers are not currently members of the audience, they must first be found before they can be studied. This, of course, is much more difficult to accomplish, but it can be done. Sometimes it may need professional assistance from a marketing researcher, but small-scale studies can be conducted, even by organisations not sufficiently funded to hire professional researchers. The cultural organisation needs to determine where these non-attenders associate and go where they are in order to conduct the research. Such locations might include clubs/associations, community groups or universities.

Research: What is it Good For?

Here are some ideas:

- *To learn more about the organisation, its competition, environment, and audience.*
- *To learn why recent successes and failures happened.*
- *To reduce risk and waste when decisions have to be made.*
- *To better position the organisation by learning about changes in demand and preference.*

Source: Chen-Courtin, 1998.

CLASSIFICATIONS OF RESEARCH

Once the research question has been decided upon, the organisation must choose a method. But first, it must decide what type of research to conduct. The cultural organisation has several types of research processes available, including descriptive, exploratory or causal. The type chosen will depend on the research question and will affect the choice of research method.

Descriptive Studies

The cultural organisation will perform a descriptive study when it needs to obtain specific data on its audience. A descriptive study is used when facts are needed. The method used to conduct descriptive studies is almost always surveys. These surveys are called quantitative studies, because they collect statistical data.

Quantitative research consists almost entirely of surveys where respondents answer predetermined questions, with answers such as "Yes" or "No" or "Frequently" or "Never". The advantage of a quantitative study is that, if the number of people surveyed (the sample) is large enough, it can be said that a fact has been proved and is true of the entire group. Quantitative studies can give answers such as "37% of the audience is over the age of 55" or "52% of the audience attends twice a year". If the number of people asked to complete the survey is large enough compared to the total group under study, the answer can even be said to be proved.

The difficulty cultural organisations have in conducting surveys is that it can be expensive and time-consuming. If the organisation wants to "prove" something, such as the percentage of older audience members, it must survey a sufficiently large number of individuals to ensure that the sample is statistically valid, which can be costly in both financial and staff resources.

Despite this difficulty, many cultural organisations have relied heavily on surveys as their only means of market research. This is unfortunate, because the type of information that surveys can provide is limited. There is also a growing problem in obtaining responses to the traditional survey. Because everyone is so pressed for time, it is now difficult to get people to respond to a survey in person, over the phone or by mail. If surveys are left on seats or at the entry or exit point of the venue, few audience members will bother to fill them out. Surveys conducted over the Internet are limited to obtaining responses from only those people who are online.

For all surveys, the people who are most likely to respond are those individuals who are most motivated to give their opinion because they are already involved with the organisation. What is needed most is the opinions of those who are not regular attenders and they are the least likely to complete a survey form.

What to do During the Interval? Research!

Why not conduct observational research every time you have an arts event? Take 10 minutes to just observe your audience and ask the questions below. Watch at a number of events and on different days/nights and see whether your answers vary.

- *What do you see? Singles – Families – Couples – Groups?*
- *Are they reading your programme?*
- *Are they noticing the artwork on the walls?*
- *Are they discussing the art or other subjects?*
- *Are they able to get to the bar?*
- *Is there a line at the toilet?*

If you can, talk with the audience and conduct informal interviews. Make a point of asking different types of people questions such as:

- *How did you hear about this event?*
- *Why did you decide to come today?*
- *How do you like this show compared with others?*
- *Where else do you attend?*

Keep this up and you soon will have your own internal database about your audience!

Source: ArtsMarketing, 2004.

Exploratory Studies

The cultural organisation should conduct an exploratory study when the research question deals with feelings, values or motivation. Such exploratory research can be useful when there is not a specific problem to investigate, but the organisation is simply trying to determine whether there are any trends or changes in consumer behaviour of which it should be aware.

This type of research is called qualitative. It differs from quantitative in that it is designed to let the person being studied provide their own answers. The questions, rather than asking for facts, focus on needs, desires, preferences and values. Because so many different answers may result, statistics cannot be generated. However qualitative studies, if designed with considerable thought as to what information is wanted and how it is to be obtained, can provide invaluable information to the organisation.

A qualitative study may be very involved, time-consuming and difficult, or it can be conducted on a small scale. Either way, the information received will be rich in details and insights that will help the organisation adapt its product to meet the desires of the audience.

As noted, it is even more difficult to obtain information from those who do not attend regularly. Qualitative research is helpful in these cases. It does not treat the audience as an undifferentiated mass from which a statistically valid sample is needed, but targets the specific individuals from which the cultural organisation wants a response.

When conducting qualitative research, the emphasis is not on the size of the sample, but on the quality of the question design and the analysis of the resulting information. For example, if asked why they attend, even if each individual has a unique answer, common themes will almost always appear. By analysing the information, the responses can be grouped so that the themes can be discovered and understood. An advantage of qualitative research is that it can also be approached in low-cost ways that are available to smaller cultural organisations.

Causal Studies

If a cultural organisation wants to study the effect of a change in its product, or the success of a new promotional campaign, it will need to use causal research. Causal research is used to discover whether a change the organisation has made, or is planning to make, has had, or will have, a positive or negative effect on the audience. Research questions that require causal research have a cause and effect. For example: Will a new promotion campaign increase interest among young people? Or, is the audience purchasing more refreshments now that we have a new menu?

If the change has already happened, data might already exist to answer the question. If the cultural organisation wants to know whether attendance demographics have changed as the result of a new promotional campaign, it can check with the box office. Or it might do observational research and just study the "look" of the audience. If it wants to know whether the menu change has changed purchasing habits, it can look at the sales figure.

However this is an expensive way to learn whether the new promotions or menu are effective. It would be better if these changes were tried on a small scale first, using an experiment method to see whether public reaction will be positive or negative. Experimentation is the most frequently-used research method when a causal study is needed.

Research Purpose and Use

Study	When to Use	Example of Use
Descriptive	Use when details and numbers are needed.	Research on audience composition or attendance frequency.
Exploratory	Use when seeking insights on motivation/behaviour.	Research on reasons for attendance or attitude toward the organisation.
Causal	Use when needing to determine effect of change.	Research on effect of promotion on attendance.

RESEARCH METHODS

Once the research question has been decided upon and the research type is chosen, the next step is to choose a research method. Methods include the survey used in quantitative descriptive research. There are more research methods available for conducting exploratory research. These are usually qualitative methods and include interviews, focus groups, projective techniques, and observation. Causal research usually requires the use of experimentation.

Traditional Survey

Designing a traditional survey is a three-step process. You first must decide upon what you want to know. Then you must decide what types of questions you want to ask and, finally, how the information will be tabulated. Because it is difficult to motivate people to complete survey forms, it is important that the survey be short enough to encourage completion. Therefore, when deciding what to ask, keep the questions to a single topic, if possible. Of course, most surveys also ask for demographic information such as age, educational level, occupation, and/or income. Additional questions should only pertain to one topic such as what type of programming is preferred or frequency of attendance. It is very tempting for the organisation to include a laundry-list of questions, but unless the survey participant is very motivated to respond, the survey will probably not be completed.

Another means of increasing the likelihood of the survey being completed is by offering incentives. The incentive might be an opportunity to enter a contest, a small gift or perhaps a seating "upgrade" to a more expensive seat. In addition, a visually interesting, well designed survey will receive more responses than a boring, cluttered survey.

Once the question is written, the next step is to design the answers. Survey questions should be designed so that most of the possible answers are included in the responses. This is easy with questions that can be answered with responses such as Yes/No or Frequently/Never. If you are asking questions on attitudes, it becomes more difficult. The question might be "what was your motivation for attendance". Providing suggested answers results in the respondent being limited to these choices. This is why surveys are not the best choice for researching motivation.

After the questions and answers have been designed, they need to be tested on a few sample participants to make sure they are asking what you think they are asking. When designing a survey, it is important that the questions be worded in the everyday language that people use. The only way this can be accomplished is by testing the survey to determine whether the questions and answers are understood correctly. If a particular group is targeted that might not speak the language of the survey as their native tongue, testing the survey is even more important. (Or the survey may be offered in more than one language.)

The final step is to decide how the data will be tabulated. For a large research study, it may be necessary to have extra assistance to enter the responses into a computer database. For a small survey with few participants, a low-tech hand-counting of responses will suffice.

Sample of Traditional Survey Question

1. Are any of the statements below reasons why you attended Brooklyn Museums First Saturday tonight? (Please check)

I feel at ease with the other people here.

I find it easy to get here from home/work.

I came to hear the gospel choir.

I came to eat, drink and socialize.

I might meet new friends here.

I came for the movie.

I want to learn more about art.

My friends or family wanted to come.

I feel that total cost including food/travel is reasonable.

I came for the dancing.

Targeted Surveys

Traditional surveys are usually composed of questions that can be answered by only a limited number of responses. This is done so that the answers can be counted and expressed as percentages and statistics. However, surveys can be designed that ask open-ended questions that allow respondents to provide an answer in their own words. These surveys are more time-consuming for a participant to complete. Therefore, if this type of survey is put into the mail or left on a seat, it usually will get a low response rate. This type of survey can best be used by asking each individual participant to participate, monitoring their progress and collecting the survey form when they are done. Because this will limit the number of completed surveys, it should only be used when targeting a specific group from whom more information is needed. Another advantage of targeting is that information can be obtained from a specific group who might usually not respond.

A targeted survey might be conducted during the interval, when audience members, perhaps selected on the basis of some demographic trait such as age or ethnic group, are asked to participate. After explaining the purpose of the study and its importance, the survey-taker gives the survey to the participant on a clip-board. This allows the participant to take the survey right where they are and also allows survey-taker to keep track of their progress. Upon completion, the clip-board is reloaded with a new survey form and handed out again. The survey-taker should be able to handle three to five participants at one time.

This type of survey will not help the organisation to "prove" anything. However, the advantage of this type of surveying is that it can target a specific group and receive responses that will not be guided by any pre-designed answers.

Sample of Targeted Survey with Open-ended Questions

Art, music, dance and the visual arts are a part of everyone's culture and life. The following questions ask you where you experienced or participated in art and culture. Please answer the questions below based on your experience during the past 12 months.

Singing:
The last place I listened to singing for free was . . . .
The last place I bought a ticket to hear singing . . . .
The last place I sang in public was . . . .
The type of singing I prefer is . . . .

Focus Groups

A focus group, also sometimes called a group interview, is the process of bringing together a group of individuals, who are then encouraged to share their opinions and concerns. A formal focus group is usually conducted by an outside professional researcher, so as to exclude bias. The advantage of a focus group over a survey is that the focus group can explore an individual's first response with additional follow-up questions and obtain more in-depth information. Often, when first asked a question, people will respond with what they believe to be the correct, or appropriate, answer. Also, most people want to be polite by answering in the affirmative and with positive praise whenever possible. By putting people together in a focus group, they can be encouraged to respond to each other's comments and go beyond their first response.

Focus groups can also be used by small cultural organisations. Even if they cannot afford a focus group planned and conducted by a professional researcher, a small cultural organisation will still find value in asking a few of its customers to participate in an informal group interview held at its venue. The person moderating the group interview does not need to be a professional market researcher, but does need basic skills in listening and human relations. Often graduate students can be used for this purpose. The role of the moderator is to be noncommittal and objective and to listen and to record what the participants say. What is critical is that the moderator should help to guide the conversation by encouraging the participants to keep their comments focused on the subject, while not guiding the opinions expressed.

Small cultural organisations can use group interviews to gather information on subjects such as proposed future programming of cultural events. During the group session, programming ideas can be described and the participants' responses recorded. This information can then be used as one factor in the programming decision-making process. Other purposes for group interviews might include exploring issues such as food choice and quality, customer service and additional amenities that could be offered to customers.

Focus groups and interviews can also be used to learn how to attract non-attenders. If the organisation has a new market segment it wishes to target, it can conduct a group interview to determine what benefits they desire. This may be done by finding participants from an organisation to which this segment already belongs, such as a university, social club, or civic organisation.

Projective Techniques

Projective techniques can be used to encourage communication in interviews and focus groups or used on their own. These are techniques that elicit information in other ways than asking verbal questions. The idea is borrowed from psychology but is gaining increased use in marketing. Some simple techniques include word association, sentence completion and cartoon tests. These are creative tools that people in cultural organisations should enjoy using.

Word association is simply asking for the participant's first response to a name, photo or event. The idea is to get emotional responses, rather than intellectual. Word association can be used in focus groups, interviews or on targeted surveys.

Example of Word Association Technique

Three words that describe your experience tonight are:

☐ _____

☐ _____

☐ _____

Another technique is *sentence* or *story completion*. This technique allows the participants to frame the experience in their own words. One task might be to ask the participants to write an advertisement for the organisation that would appeal to them and their friends. Or they might be asked to construct what they consider to be an ideal performance programme.

If these ideas are too creative and difficult for the audience, they can be given sentences that they finish such as:

- The Starving Artist Gallery is _____
- The people who visit the gallery are _____
- The Starving Artist Gallery should _____

Cartoons can also be used. The cartoon set usually consists of two characters with balloons over their heads similar to comic books. One character might be saying, "Hi Alan, I was thinking of visiting the Starving Artists Gallery. Want to go?" The survey participant then puts their own answer into the second character's bubble.

Observation

Another inexpensive research method that can be used by small cultural organisations is observation. If the cultural organisation wants to know whether its customer service desk is being used, it can watch to see who approaches and who does not. Or a museum can observe the actions of specific groups of patrons, such as families or single visitors, to help the organisation to determine which areas of the venue they most use, the length of the visit and what exhibits attract the most attention. This method will often give more accurate information than surveying, as most people do not keep track of how they use their visit.

Experimentation

Experimentation is a research method used to discover how customers will react to changes in the cultural product or service. For example, if the cultural organisation wishes to try a new refreshment menu, customer service or lobby entertainment, it can try it on a small scale to see how customers react. By experimenting, it can learn its audience's preferences before the change is tried on a large scale. It is difficult to obtain this type of feedback by surveying prior to the change, as the customer will find it difficult to have an opinion on something of which they are unfamiliar or never experienced. This research is a simple way to save the cultural organisation from costly mistakes.

Research Methods

Method	Description
Traditional Survey	Used in collection of quantitative data
Targeted Survey	Used to collect answers from a specific group
Focus Groups	Use of group dynamics to draw out subjects
Projective Technique	Creative techniques to get emotional responses
Observation	Watching people's behaviour and actions
Experimentation	Action tried on a small scale and results measured

BENCHMARKING

One type of research that is often overlooked by cultural organisations is research on competitors and competing products, often referred to as benchmarking. While a focus on improving their own product is important, cultural organisations should also keep track of what other organisations are offering to consumers. The organisations benchmarked should include both other cultural organisations and other leisure businesses. This research is crucial, as it is difficult to compete without knowing what competitors are offering to consumers.

In a benchmarking study, the cultural organisation determines what other organisations are doing to meet the needs of their consumers. The study includes an analysis of the competitors' product characteristics, strategy, organisational strengths/weaknesses, and future trends.

It is important that the benchmarking study be conducted on organisations providing the appropriate competing products. For example, theatres offering contemporary plays should be benchmarked first against other theatres offering contemporary plays. But the benchmarking may also be done with a related, but not similar, type of product such as benchmarking contemporary plays with all other plays produced at non-profit theatres.

The product may also be of a related, but different, medium such as benchmarking a theatre with a cinema. Or the benchmarking can be done on organisations offering entirely different products that provide similar benefits, such as benchmarking restaurants, sporting events or other leisure activities. The cultural organisation should not make the mistake of focusing too narrowly on only similar cultural products.

The Arts as Feminine, or Why Men Would Rather Watch Sports

Why do women attend the arts and men watch sports? Traditional arts marketing has often stressed the emotional meaning of the artwork and the emotional impact it will have on the audience. This has directly appealed to women ticket purchasers or, at least, purchasers with more traditionally "feminine" perceptions.

But men react emotionally to events based on skill and competition, which is why they are attracted to sports events. But the arts also involve a high level of technical skill. A separate marketing message might be necessary to sell the benefit of watching highly skilled professionals perform, without stressing the emotional meaning of the art.

Source: Gainer, 1993.

Performing Benchmarking

When performing benchmarking, the cultural organisation should carefully research what features, and resulting benefits, the competitor's product offers to consumers. The purpose of the benchmarking is to determine what attracts the competing organisation's audience. The audience, of course, is attracted by the cultural product, but it is also attracted by other benefits such as the quality of service, ambience, ease of product delivery or low cost. Once the cultural organisation knows what features attract the consumer to its competitor, it can decide whether these features can be added to their own product. This research can be done by interviewing managers of the competing organisation, by attending the venue as consumers, or by interviewing the competing organisation's audience.

The cultural organisation should also analyse the strengths and weaknesses of its competitors. If the cultural organisation is a theatre that targets families with children, it should examine the strengths and weaknesses not only of other theatres, but also of other competing leisure providers, such as a local amusement park, in meeting the needs of families. If the cultural organisation feels that one of the benefits that families seek is educational opportunity, then the lack of educational opportunities at the amusement park can be exploited. The theatre should then market to families that it provides a cultural experience that is both fun and educational.

If cultural organisations discover through benchmarking that they have a strength that profit competitors do not have, such as educational content, they should not assume that this advantage will continue to exist. It is important that the cultural organisation analyse any future trends that may change the competitor's strategy. As mentioned above, profit organisations are very good at looking for market opportunities. If they discover that consumers want benefits that are provided by cultural organisations, they will also attempt to provide them.

Once the cultural organisation has completed all their research, it will understand what benefits motivate attendance at its art events. This information can then be used to modify, or at least package, the cultural product so as to increase attendance.

Research Proposal Worksheet

The first step in research is to define your research question. The more specific, the more successful will be your research. Answering the following questions will help you plan your research effort:

My question is....

_____

_____

Task	Answer	Person Responsible	Date to Complete
What will I do with the information? (research objectives)			
Where can I find existing information? (desk research)			
What method will I use to find information? (research type)			
How will I ask? (method selection)			
Who will I ask? (sample definition)			
Where will I ask? (site selection)			
What will I do with the information? (analysis and reporting)			

References

ArtsMarketing.org (2004) "Practical Lessons in Marketing" online at www.artsmarketing.org/marketingresources/tutorials.

Chen-Courtin, D. (1998) "Look Before You Leap: Some Marketing Research Basics" in *Arts Reach*, June/July.

CPAND "Quick Facts about the Arts" (2004) online at www.cpand.org/arts-culture-facts/index.

Empire, K. (2003) "Observer Writers Trade Places to Bring a First-timers Perspective to the Arts" in *The Observer*, August 24.

EUCLID "ACRONIM: Arts and Cultural Research On-Line International Matrix" (2004) online at www.euclid.info/acronmin.

Gainer, B. (1993) "The Importance of Gender to Arts Marketing" in *Journal of Arts Management, Law & Society*, September.

Kolb, B. (1999) "You Call This Fun? Response of First Time Attenders to a Classical Music Concert", Paper presented at the International Arts and Cultural Management Association, Helsinki, Finland, June.

Sayre, S. (2001) *Qualitative Research for Marketplace Research*, Sage.

Chapter Eight

THE PRODUCT & ITS DISTRIBUTION

Marketing theory was originally focused on selling tangible goods, defined as physical products that are handcrafted or manufactured; for example, a packet of crisps, a jacket or a sofa. With the growth of the service industry in the 1980s, those in charge of marketing realised that services may differ in some aspects from tangible products, but they still needed to be marketed. Therefore, marketing theory was expanded to address the unique challenges presented by the need to market service products. With the expansion of the knowledge industry, it is now understood that ideas are also products that must be marketed. In marketing theory, the word *product* can now be used to describe any combination of a tangible good, a service or an idea.

Cultural products can be thought of as just such a combination. Cultural organisations provide a service when they present a play, concert or exhibit. However, consumers attending also purchase tangible products from the organisation, such as refreshments, programmes and gift items. In addition, the cultural organisation also markets the idea of supporting the arts when it sells sponsorships.

Because culture is such a unique and complicated product, it is important to understand thoroughly how consumers perceive and categorise products, including the unique features of services. These will be discussed along with product knowledge, categories, branding, packaging and distribution. This knowledge is necessary before an effective promotion campaign can be designed.

Unique Characteristics of Services

As stated earlier, the word product is used interchangeably for tangible goods, services and ideas. Services are distinguished from tangible goods by the characteristics of intangibility, inseparability, and perishability. These characteristics add to the difficulty of marketing cultural products.

Intangibility

The performance of music, dance or theatre, or an exhibit of art or artefacts has tangible features that can be seen and heard. However cultural products more closely resemble services, because they are purchased by the consumer for the intangible benefits that seeing the performance or exhibit provides.

These intangible benefits are difficult for the cultural organisation to communicate and, therefore, to market to consumers. This is particularly true of marketing to culture consumers who do not have sufficient experience with the benefits provided by cultural events. Cultural organisations should have to choose carefully the words and images used in their marketing material to inform consumers of the benefits. Unfortunately, if not chosen properly, the words and images can reinforce the culture consumer's negative stereotypes of audience élitism and product incomprehensibility.

While a tangible good is usually produced in a centralised location and then distributed and sold elsewhere, the production and consumption of culture is often at the same location. Therefore the quality of the service product is intimately connected with the surroundings, ambience and employees at the venue where the culture is produced and consumed. The art alone is not the only component of the product noticed by consumers. They will judge the product acceptable or unacceptable based on the total experience, starting with the ticket purchase, the actual performance and concluding with the convenience and availability of transportation home.

Inseparability

Because the consumer purchases the right to experience the performance or exhibit, not the performance or exhibit itself, the tangible features of the cultural product can only be examined after purchase and are therefore said to be inseparable from purchase. Even if consumers have experienced the performance or exhibit elsewhere, each experience will be unique. This makes marketing the cultural product similar to marketing a service and also similarly difficult. Cultural organisations must market cultural experiences of which many, or even most, culture consumers are totally unfamiliar until the actual purchase.

Perishability

Because, by their nature, services cannot be stored, one of the challenges is to connect supply and demand. The cultural performance or exhibit is available for only a limited time and, if there is no audience, the opportunity to sell is lost. Product perishability presents great challenges to cultural organisations that are already operating with limited financial resources.

What Else Can Ballet Companies Sell?

Ballet may be its mission, but the New York City Ballet developed an additional product to sell. Since so many people are concerned with fitness – and who knows more about fitness than dancers? – the NYC Ballet developed the NYCB Workout DVD/Video with exercises to improve strength, flexibility and cardiovascular stamina. It has proved so popular that NYCB Workout 2 is now available!

Source: New York City Ballet, 2004.

PRODUCT KNOWLEDGE

Before consumers can make a decision to consume a product, they first need to be aware of its availability. Their awareness or knowledge level can vary from the superficial, knowing only that the product exists, to comprehensive familiarity with all the levels and types of the product.

Levels of Product Knowledge

Consumers have different levels of cultural product knowledge including product class, form, brand and features that they will use to make their attendance decision. They may be only familiar with the product class, and know that something called classical music or ballet or theatre exists. Or, if they have more knowledge, consumers may also be aware that classical music comes in various product forms such as live concerts, recorded concerts and radio broadcasts; or, for theatre that Shakespearean, contemporary drama and musical theatre exist.

The next level in product knowledge is when consumers recognise brand names. For example, if consumers wish to visit a museum, they may make their decision on which to visit based on the "brand name" of the artist or the organisation offering the exhibit. If they are very knowledgeable about the art form, they may base their decision on which specific pictures are part of the exhibit.

The levels of product knowledge on which the attendance decision is based can be described using classical music as an example. At the most superficial level, a person first must be aware that classical music exists. At the next level, they must know that, if they wish to enjoy classical music, they have the choice of different product forms. They can listen to classical music on the radio, buy and listen to a CD or attend a live performance. If they decide to attend a live performance, they must have additional knowledge of brand names of orchestras or styles of music. Individuals who are very knowledgeable about classical music would be much more concerned with the details of the programme. They would base their decision on specific features of the concert, such as musical style, composer or soloist.

Levels of Depth of Product Knowledge for Classical Music

Product Class	Product Form	Brand (live)	Features (live)
Classical Music	Live	BBC Orchestra	Baroque Composer
	Radio	Philharmonia	Contemporary Conductor
	CD	South Bank	'Pops' Concert
		Wigmore Hall	Chamber Soloist
			Choral Programme

Types of Product Knowledge

Besides levels of knowledge, consumers choose products using three different types of knowledge about a product. The cultural organisation must provide the appropriate type of knowledge needed by consumers to make their attendance decision. The first type of knowledge concerns the features of the product. Using live performances of classical music as an example, this knowledge would include such physical characteristics as performer, time and date of concert, music programming, physical attributes of the venue and additional services provided. Cultural organisations are already skilled at providing this information.

The second type of knowledge concerns the bundle of benefits, including both functional and psychosocial, that will be provided to consumers when they choose the product. These include such functional benefits as attaining additional knowledge about classical music or enjoying a social occasion. The psychosocial benefits to consumers might include an enhanced feeling of intelligence or social standing. Cultural organisations are less skilled at providing consumers with this type of information because they themselves are unsure of how consumers benefit.

The third type of knowledge needed by consumers concerns what values are associated with use of the product. Consumers may be motivated to choose to attend a live classical concert because it satisfies a personal value such as contributing to the betterment of society, increasing personal growth, or performing a ritual of one's social class.

Types of Product Knowledge of Live Classical Music

Features of Product	Benefits Provided by Product	Values Associated with Product
Programme	Opportunity to socialise	Support of arts
Performer	Increased knowledge	Self-growth
Venue amenities	Relaxation/entertainment	Social standing

Value Chain

These three levels of product knowledge can be thought of as a chain:

In a successful promotional message, the cultural organisation answers all three questions. Culture enthusiasts make the attendance decision based on values, as they are already familiar with culture's features and benefits. To influence the decision of culture consumers, the cultural organisation must first educate them as to the features of the cultural product. However they must also be convinced that they will benefit from attendance. Only after attendance can consumers learn whether a cultural event reflects their personal values.

Product Risk

Unfortunately, some values that culture enthusiasts find attractive, such as exhibiting membership in a social status group or demonstrating their cultural knowledge, may actually prove a barrier to culture consumers. Rather than being considered benefits, these values pose risks to consumers with little knowledge of the art form. These risks must be minimised if culture consumers are to be attracted. The negative risks of attending a cultural event might include:

• Feeling like an outsider or social failure.
• Enduring a boring evening.

- Having no opportunity for social contact.
- Feeling ignorant.

Forget Group Therapy, Just Go to the Opera

Between 1990 and 1995, the Canadian Opera Company, based in Toronto, lost half of its subscribers. The company realised that drastic action was needed to attract a new and younger audience. It succeeded by launching the "18 to 29: Opera for a New Age" membership promotion. For a small fee, a member received one free opera ticket, a discount at a popular music store, an opera CD, a souvenir programme and the opera newsletter.

The seats for the free ticket, and any future inexpensive tickets the member might wish to purchase, were not at the back of the balcony. They were the best unsold seats the opera had available. The result was an "explosion" in the number of young people attending the opera.

The Canadian Opera Company attributes the success of the promotion to two factors: offering good seats at reduced prices and having a cultural product that is attractive to today's media-savvy young consumer. To promote the membership scheme, the ad campaigns focused on universities, bookstores, cafes and pubs. The marketing message made no apology for opera's focus on sex and violence. An example from a brochure:

> *"Your mother and her lover have just killed your father with an axe. Your exiled brother is probably dead. People are plotting to imprison you in a dark tower. In the midst of all this, your sister just wants to settle down and have a normal family. The time for group therapy has passed. Experience the rage and fury of Electra."*

Oh by the way, the program is still going strong. Although now you don't need to be a member, just have a valid ID that proves your age. Because as the opera's website warns, it's only for the young: "No bringing your mom – get yourself a date. And she's got to be 30 too."

Source: Fanciullo and Banks, 1998; Canadian Opera Company, 2004.

CATEGORIES OF PRODUCTS

Products can be divided into convenience, comparison and speciality products, based on how the product is purchased and used by the consumer. The different categories of products require different promotional messages.

Convenience Products

Convenience products are routinely purchased by consumers and very little thought or research goes into the purchase decision. Convenience products are usually low-cost for the consumer and low-profit for the producer. Because of the low profit, producers can only make money by selling in volume and, therefore, convenience products are designed to appeal to a broad range of consumers and are distributed widely to reach a large market. The promotional message for convenience products focuses on cost and convenience. Typical convenience products are soft drinks, fast food and toothpaste which are quickly consumed.

Comparison Products

Comparison products last longer once purchased and have a higher price than convenience products. Consequently, consumers will spend time comparison-shopping and researching the product before the purchase is made. The features offered by comparison products are usually fairly consistent across brands. When this is true, consumers will make the purchase decision based on price and, only secondly, on features. For example, a refrigerator is a standard, basic appliance and therefore price variance between products will be an important factor in the purchase decision. But the lowest-priced refrigerator must also be convenient in terms of purchase location and product delivery. If consumers have to spend too much additional time and energy on making the purchase and getting the product home, these factors will negate the lower price.

If the comparison product offers a choice of features, consumers will approach the purchase decision differently. For example, when choosing an automobile, even though all autos perform the same function, the decision of which model to purchase will often first be based on features such as design, size and power, and only then on price. Consumers may even spend more money than they anticipated in order to receive the desired features. Therefore, the promotional message for comparison products focuses on features and their benefits.

Speciality Products

Speciality products have unique features or a unique brand identity. Consumers will not accept substitutes when they decide to purchase a speciality product. An example is a Rolex watch, which performs the same function and has similar features as other expensive brands. Nevertheless consumers purchase the Rolex because they consider other brands unacceptable. The promotion message for speciality products focuses on image, not features.

COMPARISON OF DIFFERENT CULTURAL PRODUCTS

Culture may also be described as a convenience, comparison or speciality product depending on the type of art form, whether it is considered high or popular culture and the market segment targeted. The category of product will also depend on how the art form is presented. Understanding how a consumer categorises the cultural product can help with the designing of an effective promotional message.

Culture as a Convenience Product

If culture is sold as a convenience product, with wide distribution and low cost, it will almost always contain at least some elements of popular culture. To sell the product at low cost, and still gain sufficient revenue requires a cultural product that will appeal to a broad range of consumers. Companies selling "convenience" culture are willing to make the necessary compromises in designing the product so that it appeals to the wider public. Sometimes these cultural convenience products may be of a lesser quality, but consumers will still purchase them because of the low cost and easy availability.

Organisations working with high culture are often unwilling or unable to make the compromises in quality necessary to appeal to a broad public. Because of their focus on producing art of the highest quality, they are also unable to lower the cost of their product. Their mission requires them to have the best (and most expensive) artists and performers. Because they are not able to change their product to attract the mass public, they cannot earn anywhere near sufficient revenue to cover costs and must rely on outside financial support. The lack of wide public appeal and sufficient revenue results in the cultural organisation, even though it has a high quality product, being unable to distribute its product more widely. For these reasons, high culture can rarely be sold as a convenience product.

The Cultural Consumer Goes to the Opera

Raymond Gubbay has been producing classical concerts in the UK for over 30 years – without subsidy. He now promotes over 600 concert and opera performances a year.

He pioneered the "classical music experience" concerts, which feature laser and light shows along with the music. He also has pioneered producing opera for the masses. In 1998, he produced Madame Butterfly *at the Royal Albert Hall. The opera was promoted to the general public and received no government funding. The result? 80,000 people in just 15 performances saw the opera.*

Source: Tilden, 2001.

Culture as a Comparison Product

If consumers lack knowledge about art and culture, they will consider the cultural event a comparison product. They will believe that any cultural event is substitutable with any other form of cultural event because, to such consumers, all the events have similar features and provide similar benefits. Therefore, when deciding between specific performances or exhibits, consumers will attend the lowest-priced and most convenient alternative that meets their needs. The majority of culture consumers fall into this category.

However culture enthusiasts are knowledgeable about culture and will decide that they are willing to pay more for a specific feature, such as a particular performer or a visit to a specific exhibit. They will also be willing to travel and arrange their schedule so they can attend the performance or exhibit; even if the location and time are inconvenient. Both high culture and popular culture can be marketed as comparison products.

Multi-tasking at the Concert

How do you attract busy young professionals to classical music when they may be unfamiliar with the product and they don't have the time or interest in attending the usual pre-concert lecture?

The "Concert Companion" may be the way. It's a personal digital assistant (PDA) that silently provides information about what you are hearing while the concert is going on. The information is synchronized with the music so that you can know exactly what the next movement is about.

"Won't it be distracting?" critics ask. Probably not for young professionals who routinely multi-task every other moment of their lives!

Source: NPR, 2003.

Culture as a Speciality Product

Culture enthusiasts view culture as a speciality product and have a specific brand preference. They will not accept substitutes and will incur additional expense and inconvenience to purchase the product. When enthusiasts wish to see Caravaggio paintings and will not accept substitutes, the only acceptable product is a Caravaggio exhibition. Culture enthusiasts may also view the cultural event as a speciality product because of the brand name. If they desire to attend an opera at the Royal Opera House, the same opera, performed elsewhere, will not be acceptable. Culture consumers will not go to this trouble because they do not perceive the importance of a specific brand.

Want to Know What Non-attenders Think?
Ask Your Art Ambassadors

"We often get one chance to reach out to a new audience and the quality of that initial relationship can have a critical impact" according to Phil Cave, Director of Audience and Market Development. This quote is from a guide on using 'arts ambassadors'. These ambassadors are people belonging to the new group being targeted as future audience members such as an ethnic minority or the elderly. The ambassador provides communication both to the targeted group about the art form but also to the organisation about what the audience thinks. The organisation may not hear what they want, but they will hear what they need to learn to make the experience better so the audience returns.

Source: Art Audiences, 2003.

BRANDING

Branding is becoming an issue of increasing interest to cultural organisations. Branding is defined as the visible identity of the product that represents the product in the public's mind. This identity consists of the cultural organisation's name, logo, slogan or combination of all three. The brand is not the product, but is designed to evoke the product's benefits in the mind of the consumer. Use of the brand then serves as a shortcut in communication between the organisation and the public. As it is difficult to market art because its benefits are intangible, branding can be particularly useful to cultural organisations as a means of distinguishing their product from others in the mind of the consumer. This package of product plus benefits is what makes the organisation distinctive and in marketing is referred to as the USP or unique selling proposition.

What Constitutes Brand Identity?

When considering how to brand a cultural organisation it is important to understand the elements of brand identity. There are five components that need to be identified:

- *Brand loyalty: Does your organisation have a strong percentage of repeat visitors?*

- *Brand awareness: Does your potential audience know who you are and what you do?*

- *Perceived quality: Are you best at what matters to your audience?*

- *Brand associations: What other types of products does your audience associate you with?*

- *Proprietary assets: Besides your core cultural product, what else are you known for?*

Source: Caldwell, 1999.

Of course, brand identity lets a consumer know that an opera company produces opera and that an art gallery exhibits art. However brand identification goes beyond identifying the tangible elements of the product and allows organisations to distinguish their cultural product from other cultural products by denoting its intangible features. Such features could be the excitement of live theatre, the grandeur of classical music or the edginess of contemporary visual art.

In addition, cultural organisations can also use branding to align their product more closely with other types of similar products that may be attractive to consumers. Such benefits as the social aspects of the evening and how they will be entertained can be communicated with the brand. This allows them to inform the consumer as to the type of experience they are going to have. If the consumer enjoys the experience, they will then identify their enjoyment with the brand name and consume the product on a repeat basis. When a product is intangible, it is even more important that there is a brand identity for the cultural organisation.

A cultural organisation needs to be aware that it will be branded, even without the organisation's active involvement. The branding of the cultural organisation's product is created in the public's mind through word-of-mouth, stories in the media and general advertising. When these reinforce negative stereotypes, the branding works to the detriment of the organisation.

BBC "Brands" the Proms

According to research, the BBC Henry Wood Promenade Concerts have excelled in establishing a brand image and customer loyalty. The Proms, established in 1895 with Sir Henry Wood as conductor, is a series of over 70 classical concerts that takes place every summer in London. When asked why they attended, the audience's response indicated a clear pattern.

The three top-ranked reasons – low ticket price, informality and quality of performance – were far in front of the other 10 ranked reasons. Low price, informality and quality are part of all Proms concerts and could be said to be what constitutes the Proms "brand".

Because of their brand image, audience members will choose to attend a programme being performed at the Proms while they will not attend the same programme performed by another organisation.

Source: Kolb, 1997.

THE CULTURAL PRODUCT PACKAGE

The cultural product is more than merely the performance and/or object that is produced by the artist. The cultural product is the complete package of the performance/object, along with everything else the experience has to offer. This includes additional features such as lobby entertainment or educational lectures. In addition it also includes the physical surroundings, social atmosphere and the customer service. The cultural product is in actuality always an "event", even if it is only a visual arts display and not a three-day Celtic music festival.

This is because products consist of more than just the item or service that is provided. The cultural product has a primary core product, the performance or exhibit, which the organisation provides to the consumer. This core product should be seen as only the central element, which then must be packaged.

"Send the Tux to the Cleaners and Leave it there"

Oregonians love their beer. So Fortissimo, the Oregon Symphony's association developed to initiate young professionals into classical music, designed the "Chamber Music on Tap" series. What exactly is Fortissimo? It's described as a "social activity. It's a volunteer group. It's an educational resource. It's a networking opportunity. It's whatever you choose to make it".

The concerts are held in a historic warehouse that has been converted into a brewery. Audience members can socialize, interact with the musicians, drink great beer and enjoy classical music – all at the same time.

What young professional wouldn't want to attend?

Source: Oregon Symphony, 2004.

Packaging the Cultural Product as an Event

Packaging is usually thought of as the paper or container in which a tangible product is purchased. The package is designed to protect the product, but also to assist in creating the product's brand identity. Different packaging can be used to make the same product appeal to different consumers.

Cultural products are intangible services, but they can also be thought of as being packaged. Rather than surrounding the cultural product with foil or foam, the product is packaged with additional services and events. The core product of the play, concert or exhibit without "packaging" would be just as difficult to sell as a book without a cover. Of course serious readers understand that "you can't tell a book by its cover" but culture consumers use the cover to decide whether they will even pick up the book.

For this reason, it is especially difficult to attract culture consumers and fans to the cultural product without exciting packaging. The packaging they desire might be lobby entertainment, unique food and beverages and distinctive décor. A successful package also includes intangibles such as the ambience and staff attitudes that are designed to attract culture consumers. All of this packaging together creates a "buzz" of excitement as soon as the cultural consumer enters the door.

The same cultural product can be packaged differently for culture enthusiasts. The packaging that will attract them will include additional features that will meet their needs to socialise with others who are knowledgeable about the art form. This packaging might include pre-concert lectures, extensive programme notes and opportunities to meet the artists.

Other packaging that would attract enthusiasts would be an opportunity to become more involved with the art form and cultural organisation by becoming sponsors or the opportunity to volunteer for the organisation. This type of packaging not only provides assistance and support for the cultural organisation, it also helps to develop the relationship with the organisation and helps the cultural organisation fulfil its mission by becoming more closely involved with the members of the community.

Who's an Artist? Everyone!

What happens when everyone who wants to, gets to be an artist? New creative software has joined the traditional creative tools necessary for artwork, such as paint, paper, and clay, which have always been available. But the missing ingredient has been access to an audience. Now with the Internet, the audience is just a homepage away. Teenagers are particularly interested in producing web pages, probably because creativity helps in the process of constructing their own identity. Does this make them artists? Who's to say? According to artist Amy Bruckman:

> *"The Net is not a place for 'professionals' to publish and the masses to merely download. Online, everyone is becoming an artist: everyone is a creator. The network is providing new opportunities for self-expression, and demands a new kind of artist: the artistic instigator, someone who inspires other people to be creative by setting a positive example with their own work, and providing others with tools, context, and support. That support can be technical, aesthetic, or emotional – encouraging others to believe in their own capabilities and take the risk of trying to make something personally meaningful.... Online, it's true you can download paintings from the Louvre – but much more interesting is the fact that you can upload your own. Or better yet, inspire others to do so."*

Source: Bruckman, 1999.

DISTRIBUTION OF CULTURE

The distribution system for cultural products has been a non-issue for most cultural organisations. The cultural event has usually been held in a traditional venue such as a performance hall, museum or gallery. When cultural organisations have considered the problem of the distribution of culture, their response has been to send the event on tour to other traditional venues in the belief that it is only geographic distance that keeps consumers from attending. But it may be the traditional venue itself that keeps consumers away.

A new approach to cultural distribution is to understand that it is as much psychic distance as physical distance that keeps consumers from attending. If the audience is not willing to come to the venue, there is no reason why the cultural product cannot be brought to the audience. The distribution of culture to new types of venues to increase attendance is being tried by adventurous cultural organisations. The approaches they use vary as to the type of organisation and art form, but include taking the art form into non-traditional venues such as shopping malls, churches and dance clubs. Consumers are much more likely to attend a concert, play or exhibit for the first time when it is in a venue with which they are already familiar.

What if You Have No Venue?

The Taft Museum of Art in Cincinnati was forced to close its doors for necessary renovations in 2001 for over two years. The museum had two choices: to announce to the public its closure or to stay open via the Internet and other venues. The museum decided to stay in business even though it's building was closed. How?

- *It offered a virtual tour online.*
- *It opened a 'museum within a museum' showing part of its collection at another art museum.*
- *All programmes including slide talks, chamber music series and art camp continued at other venues including libraries, restaurants and even a bell factory.*

Did it work? During the first nine months it was closed, the museum served 26,000 people (not counting the visitors to the 'museum within a museum').

During the same time period a year before, when it was open, it served 37,000. Thus it continued to serve the public despite being without its own venue. Amazingly it only lost 90 museum members over the two years.

Source: Roberts, 2002.

The Non-traditional Venue

If the mission of a cultural organisation is to expose as many people as possible to its art, it makes sense to take the art where the people are. One way to accomplish this is take a sample of the art or the complete product out of the traditional venue. While it is common for arts organisations to take their work to schools, there are many other possible venues in the community. Chamber groups could perform in public venues such as the lobbies of corporate headquarters during lunch break. This could even be part of their rehearsal process. Museums and galleries could exhibit in restaurants, businesses or stores. Of course, this is an opportunity for the organisation to communicate to the audience how they can experience more of the art through regular attendance. The cultural organisation might be surprised at how interested businesses are in incorporating art into their physical environment.

Airports are getting into the Museum Business

The San Francisco Airport has so many exhibits ranging from Haitian voodoo art to displays of Tiffany glass to African-American quilts, that it has a position of Director and Chief Curator. Why art at the airport? It's free, it's open 24 hours and people are stuck there waiting for the plane anyway. So why not provide the opportunity to enjoy viewing some art?

Are the exhibits any good? They have to be! According to Blake Summers, the current curator,

> *"We have been very much in the vanguard in trying to humanize these large public spaces. People are not going to the airport to see an exhibition, so we have to attract the attention of this audience as they walk by. We catch a much broader range of people than any museum."*

Source: McDonnell, 2003.

Building Community: The Third Place

Cultural organisations should think of their venue as more than just places to view art. They can also serve the purpose of building community. Everyone needs what is called a "Third Place" (Oldenburg, 1999). This is a place besides work and home, where we can associate with others. It allows for informal public life, where different types of people can connect as equals. Historically, these places have been the local coffee shop, bookstore or barber. But today more people commute long distances and, when they do get home, they tend to retreat behind their own front door.

Society needs a place that is a friendly "leveller", where people from different social positions can come together because of a shared interest. People are social animals and one of the main reasons for arts attendance is a social experience. Unfortunately, cultural organisations sometimes misperceive this need to socialise as frivolous and of secondary importance. And yet it is a basic human need and helping people to maintain social connections is an important contribution to the community.

Does Anybody Really Notice the Toilets?

Oh yes they do! An example is given on the Artsmarketing.org website of a theatre that suffered an unexpected loss in season ticket holders. After lots of research, a staff member discovered the problem accidentally while standing in line for the women's restroom. The problem: only two toilets and one had been broken for over a year.

So, the theatre rehabbed the existing toilets and even added new ones. It then sent a letter to each season ticket holder informing them of the improvements and offering a three-ticket package for the rest of the season.

Result: It regained 90% of its lapsed subscribers. Clean toilets do make a difference!

Source: Artsmarketing.org, 2004.

Welcoming Visitors

To have the kind of atmosphere that encourages people to connect and build community, both the venue and the organisation must be welcoming. The cultural organisation should treat each visitor as if they were a visitor to its own home. This includes maintaining a clean environment and having useful signage so people can find their way. The organisation should see that there are comfortable seating areas in the lobby where people can relax and enjoy each other's company. If refreshments are served, there should be tables available on which to put the glasses down. And, of course, it should provide adequate toilet facilities. A few fresh flowers on the ticket counter, or in the ladies rest room, would communicate that the organisation cares how it is perceived by the public.

Also, just as when friends are invited home, the organisation must be friendly and welcoming to its customers to put them at their ease. It is better to meet customers with a smile and friendly greeting rather than with just a hand out for the ticket. Even better would be to remember the names of regular visitors and greet them personally.

Building Community: Technology

Rather than merely bemoan the changes in cultural consumption habits caused by technology, cultural organisations can use them to involve the individual and the community in the artistic process. Cultural organisations, which have always been believers in community outreach, can use technology to help build a community with the public as equal partners. The new information technologies, such as email and the Internet, provide cultural organisations with new possibilities to build this partnership by reaching segments of the public, such as the disabled and ethnic minorities, which have been difficult to attract to the venue itself.

Now technology has taken the relationship one step closer toward equality. Members of the public who feel they are also creative now have the option of actually creating art themselves and finding their own audience. Of course, not everyone is doing so. But the young, who are the culture consumers that organisations need to attract, feel that this ability puts them on an equal footing with artists. They may not create art of the same quality, but still consider themselves to be creative. This should make these young culture consumers more, not less, receptive to art. However it will make them absolutely unwilling to be dictated to by cultural organisations.

Fortunately technology provides cultural organisations with a new means of reaching out online to groups not attending and to the young. Young people especially are very comfortable working with computers and cultural organisations can use this familiarity to produce online resources that interest them at the same time as they teach them to enjoy the art form and help them become part of the arts community – not just attenders.

A thorough understanding of how products are perceived and consumed can help a cultural organisation package their product to be more attractive to new target market segments. In addition, rethinking how they distribute culture can result in bringing art closer to these groups.

Product Worksheet

We offer the following core art product:

Product	Description	Benefits it Offers

Our core product could be packaged as the following events to attract different target markets: i.e. singles nights, family activities, educational opportunities, tours, outreach, etc.

Event Description	Market Segment Targeted	Benefits Offered

Here is how we need to improve the physical packaging of our product:

	Description	Suggested Improvements
Comfort		
Design		
Cleanliness		
Signage		
Furnishings		
Toilets		

Our product brand is unique because (Unique Selling Proposition or USP):

_____

_____

_____

Place Worksheet

Answer these questions on how to maximise your venue's potential:

Question	Description	Suggested Improvements
How does our location affect your attendance?		
Does the appearance of our building attract attendance?		
What is the public transportation/parking situation?		
What about cross-promotions with neighbouring business?		
How can walk- and drive-by traffic be attracted?		
How does our website provide location information?		
Where else can we distribute our product?		

References

Arts Audiences (2003) "Making the Most of Arts Ambassadors" online at www.newaudiences.org.uk/static/news_story_20031201_2.

ArtsMarketing.org (2004) "Practical Lessons in Marketing" online at www.artsmarketing.org/marketingresources/tutorials.

Bruckman, A. (1999) "Cyberspace is not Disneyland: The Role of the Artist in a Networked World" in *Epistemology and the Learning Group: MIT Media Lab*, online at: www.ahip.getty.edu/cyberpub/bruckman.html, May.

Caldwell, N.G. (1999) "Brand Identify and Museum Marketing" in Proceedings, 5th International Conference on Arts and Cultural Management, June.

Canadian Opera Company (2004) "18to29: Opera for a New Age" online at www.coc.ca/tickets/18to29.

Fanciullo, D. and Banks, A. (1998) "Surge of Popularity Creates a New Age for Opera" *Arts Reach*, September.

Kolb, B. (1997) "Redefining the Classical Music Concert: Why Audiences Love the BBC Proms" in *Arts Reach*, September, Volume V, Issue 10.

New York City Ballet (2004) online at www.nycballet.com/programs/workout.

NPR (2003) "A Digital Companion for Concert Fans: Classical Program Notes go the Way of the PDA" online at www.npr.org/features.php?wfld=1434167.

Oldenburg, R. (1999) *The Great Good Place: Cafes, Coffee Shops, Bookstores, Bars, Hair Salons and Other Great Hangouts at the Heart of a Community*, Marlowe & Company.

Oregon Symphony (2004) online at www.orsymphony.org/fortissimo.

Roberts, J. (2002) "What to do When the Doors Temporarily Close" in *Arts Reach*, December.

Tilden, I. (2001) "Let Me Entertain You" in *Guardian Unlimited* online at www.guardian.co.uk/Archive/Article/0,4273,4314114,00.

Chapter Nine

PRICING & FUNDING AS REVENUE SOURCES

Too often cultural organisations have thought of marketing as only promotion. However to develop marketing strategy means also considering the pricing of the product. Of course, pricing is complicated for non-profit organisations because they also rely on funding from additional sources other than from customers. However, pricing theory is important to understand because the more revenue that can be obtained directly from customers, the less time and effort will need to be put into other means of raising revenue.

This does not mean that cultural organisations will be able to price their product so no outside funding is needed. If they could, they would then be a for-profit business. But the days when cultural organisations could ignore the basics of pricing theory are gone. Pricing strategy can even be used to motivate attendance to the art event. Therefore an understanding of the cost, competition and value approach to pricing can be used to motivate attendance.

PRICING

Cultural organisations rarely compete on price. Instead, they use non-price competition by stressing the quality of the product. This is also a common practice for profit organisations that sell speciality products that have no easy substitutes. Because the consumer cannot find other similar products to compare prices, they usually accept the stated price as correct. However that does not mean they are willing to pay the price. Cultural organisations usually respond to this refusal to purchase by lowering the price believing that the consumer is unable to afford to attend. However, the refusal to purchase is often because the price is unacceptable considering the perceived value, not because the customer lacks the ability to pay. In fact, lowering the price may not inspire a purchase but have the opposite effect as it sends the psychological message that the product is not worth the price.

Why Does it Cost so Much to Go to the Opera?

The San Diego Opera tackled this question two ways. First they slashed rush ticket prices by $15 to $20 for last minute purchasers and sold three-opera subscription packages starting at only $60. But they also communicated directly to the public on their website:

> *"The cost of tickets to performing arts events, like anything else, is relative. Opera is the most expensive performing art form to create, combining as it does all the elements of a large stage production and an orchestra concert, and presenting world-class opera singers, conductors and director. Keep in mind that although your opera ticket may seem expensive, the amount you paid for it actually covers only 55% of what it costs us to produce the opera."*

Sources: Scher, 2002 and San Diego Opera, 2004.

Cost Pricing

When thinking about pricing, one of the first issues that marketing must consider is the actual cost of producing the product. For a profit business, the price charged for a product must at least cover the cost of production. If not, the company will sooner or later have to close its doors because it will not be able to pay its bills. Hopefully, the company is able to price their product to cover costs and also provide a healthy profit. This profit could be reinvested in the company, set aside to cover any future costs, or be paid out to the employees, owners or stockholders.

Cultural organisations, being non-profits, may never be able to cover the costs of producing their product through revenue from purchases alone. Even if they were able to, because of their non-profit status, any extra revenue above cost would need to be reinvested in the accomplishing the organisation's mission.

However, this does not mean that the practice of pricing to cover the cost of the product is unimportant for cultural organisations. After all, the more money that is made from purchase revenue, the less time and money the organisation will need to spend on fundraising.

The cost of a product is calculated by determining the fixed and variable costs. The fixed costs of any organisation, profit or non-profit, are the costs that would be have to be paid even if no product is produced at all. For example, the organisation must still pay rent or mortgage for its premises even if it does not mount a production. This is the reason why small cultural organisations do not maintain expensive offices or permanent galleries or theatres.

It will also have the cost of any payments for equipment, whether purchased or rented, that is necessary to produce its product. This includes office equipment such as computers and copying machines. It also includes production equipment, such as special lighting for theatres or galleries.

Another fixed cost that must be covered is administrative staff needed to run the organisation even when no play or exhibit is taking place. Therefore the smaller the administrative staff, the less dependent the organisation will be on generating revenue.

Once the organisation has determined its fixed costs, the next step is to calculate the variable costs. Variable costs are those that vary depending on how much or what type of cultural product is produced. For a theatre company, variable costs might be payment for the right to produce a play, the cost of the actors and director and the cost of marketing the play. For a gallery, the variable costs would include the cost of mounting a specific show. Variable costs will differ for every organisation and for each type of production within each organisation.

If a cultural organisation could work out the cost of all fixed and variable costs, it could use the "breakeven formula". The breakeven point is the number of tickets it would need to sell at a certain price to cover all costs. The calculation is simple:

Breakeven Point

$$\frac{\text{Fixed Costs}}{(\text{Price} - \text{Variable Costs per Person})}$$

If the organisation decides that it would be unable to ever sell that many tickets, it has three choices. Raise the price, lower the costs or obtain more money through fundraising.

However, it is very difficult even for profit businesses to determine the cost of a service. This is because it is difficult to determine the variable cost of the product for each person who attends. It is much easier to use this formula if an organisation is producing a tangible product, such as a table, where the variable costs would be the cost of the wood and the labour to assemble.

Competition Pricing

Unfortunately, the difficulty in calculating the actual costs of producing the arts product has led some cultural organisations to believe the only method for deciding a price is to just randomly choose. However there are other pricing methods that can be used. One of the simplest is to use your competition as a guide. This is a marketing, rather than a production, approach to pricing. This is because the assumption is made that the consumer has money to attend. Therefore, they will not make the decision on what activity to pursue based on price unless your price is dramatically different than the other competing products under consideration.

This is why it is so important for cultural organisations to understand who consumers consider as their competition. To use this pricing concept, the cultural organisation should check the price charged by other similar arts organisations in their area. They should also check the price of other competing leisure activities. This might mean that the cultural organisation should price their product in line with the cost of a cinema ticket, or the price of an evening in the pub. A different cultural organisation might consider its competition to be a more expensive evening out, such as a dinner and dancing, and price accordingly.

However, even when using this approach, the organisation still must consider its costs. The further the price they charge is from the theoretical price that would allow the organisation to cover all costs (the breakeven point), the more reliant the organisation will be on fundraising.

Are People Willing to Pay for Friendship?

Yes! To join friends at the National Concert Hall in Dublin costs €100 but they still have attracted 1,000 members. How? By providing members with benefits such as discount concert vouchers, friend's hospitality desk at concerts, free programmes and special offers on CD's. But also important are the social benefits. According to Rosita Wolfe, marketing manager:

> *"It's a good basis for people to come regularly to the concert hall to be part of a club."*

And socialization is a benefit for which they are willing to pay!

Sources: Moloney, 2003.

Prestige Pricing

There is a third method of pricing. Cultural organisations rarely focus on price when promoting their products but rather on the benefits and quality that will be received. The most thought they have given to pricing is to ensure that their price compares well with the price charged by their competition. However for some arts events, even the price charged by the competition is not relevant. These are speciality arts products for which there is no easily obtained substitute. In this case, the cultural organisation can price high and still attract attendance. Examples of such events are blockbuster shows of Impressionist art or operas with star performers. Fundraising galas and opening nights are other examples.

Consumers are willing to pay high prices for these events because they know that they will be given the opportunity to consume a product that is rarely available. Besides the product, they are also obtaining the status of attending such an event. In these cases, a low price might even send the wrong message to the public and discourage attendance.

COMBINING PRICING METHODS

Of course, there is no reason why a cultural organisation must use only one approach to pricing. An organisation might use cost pricing when deciding what to charge for refreshments, as the organisation does not want to use revenue from fundraising to subsidise the cost of refreshments. Therefore, it must know the fixed costs to staff the bar and also the variable cost of the refreshments. It can even charge more than the breakeven point to help cover the cost of producing the art product. The same is true of any related merchandise such as coffee mugs and t-shirts, that are available.

At the same time the organisation might use competition pricing when deciding upon the regular ticket or admittance price. In addition for special events the organisation would also use prestige pricing.

Differential Pricing

Another way to combine pricing methods is to have different ticket or admittance prices for different groups, times or events. The organisation might have student or senior pricing. It might also consider family or group pricing. Differential pricing can be used to price events differently based on demand. If Thursday is a slow day at the museum, the cost can be lowered to attract additional demand. This is done because the museum's fixed costs of having the doors open remains, no matter how many people come through the door. So any increase in attendance, even at a lower price, will help to offset costs. Likewise, the organisation might have different prices for day or evening performances.

EXTERNAL SOURCES OF REVENUE

Money has always been a critical issue for cultural organisations and the continual need to search for revenue affects the manner in which cultural organisations are managed. The main sources of money are revenue from sales of tickets and related merchandise to customers and funding from the government, corporations and wealthy patrons. All of these revenue sources have a vested interest in the type of cultural product produced. As a result, the search for funding also affects the marketing strategy for the organisation.

Historically, the main financial support for artists and the arts was provided by either the royal courts or the church. The relationship between the courts or church and the artist during the 16th and 17th centuries was not based on altruism, but on the use of art for political propaganda, a way to display power and wealth and as a means to compete (Hogwood, 1977).

As cities, and then government bodies, took over providing funding for cultural organisations, the rationale was similar. Arts was used as a means of competition between rival cities. A high level of artistic quality was sought, not as an end in itself or to better serve the audience, but with the aim of beating the competition. This is still true, particularly in describing the funding of cultural organisations located in the international capitals of the world. The government support of these organisations often has had more to do with attracting tourists and large corporate headquarters to the city than with promoting the art form itself.

Rationale for Public Funding

Despite recent cutbacks, cultural organisations do continue to receive government funding. A modern, pragmatic rationale for this continuing support for culture by the taxpayers is that cultural organisations supplement the educational offerings of the schools. Another pragmatic argument is that cultural organisations provide economic and employment benefits to the community and can also be used as a focal point for urban regeneration.

Support of public funding also continues to be defended because cultural organisations provide a community with increased status. Of course, this is the same argument made for the funding of sports teams and sports arenas. There is also the very traditional and deeply felt belief by many that the arts should be supported by the public because it is a civilising influence, an argument that the supporters of football cannot match.

However this traditional argument that art should be funded because it helps make the world a better place is becoming increasingly difficult to sell to taxpayers. As a result, the argument has changed its emphasis from a general improvement of society to more specific benefits. However, it is still the same argument in a different form.

It Sounds Good ... But Will it Work?

According to author Joli Jensen, the response to taxpayers' complaints about funding the arts has been to find a number of rationales:

> *"So how can arts supporters respond to hostility from people who resent being told that stuff they don't understand, don't like, and often find offensive is still good for them and for America, and should be funded by tax dollars? They found ways, however vaguely, to redefine the arts as a creative continuum and creative heritage.*
>
> *"According to a typical example of art-booster literature, the Campaign to Triple California State Funding to the Arts, support for the arts is about support for self-expression, healing, wisdom, diversity, growth, safer neighborhoods, drug rehabilitation, and higher property values."*

Unfortunately, tax revenue fell in California (which has the sixth largest economy in the world) and the funding of art was slashed from $18 million to $1 million. I guess the message didn't work!

Sources: Jensen, 2002 and Washington Times, 2002.

CORPORATE SPONSORSHIP

Because of the increasing difficulty in obtaining funding, cultural organisations no longer just look to the government. Another source used by cultural organisations is corporate sponsorship. The cultural organisation and corporation negotiate an agreement with benefits for both. The cultural organisation provides both visibility for the corporate name and entertainment options for the corporation's employees and guests, while the corporation provides funding and other support. Not everyone involved with cultural organisations approves of this collaboration between art and business, as such collaborations can be seen as potentially contaminating the purity of the arts. In fact, some believe the danger exists that, if corporations sponsor the arts, the corporation will start making demands on what art is presented.

Nevertheless despite these fears, as government support of cultural organisations has declined, interest in corporate sponsorship has grown. The resulting sponsorship agreements are not just about gaining funds to cover operational expenses or even special projects. Corporate sponsorship has now become the fastest growing form of marketing for cultural organisations (Field, 1999).

What is Sponsorship?

"A broad term that covers many kinds of business/non-profit relationships from financial to in-kind operational support. Non-profit organisations can create innovative sponsorship opportunities of many different kinds to engage additional corporate partners, reach wider audiences, increase financial support, or build operations and strategic capacity. Many levels and types of sponsorships are often developed to create opportunities at various financial or in-kind contribution levels... The key is to have clearly defined responsibilities, often in a written agreement, and policies that ensure a sponsorship is consistent with the company's and the non-profit's mission, business strategy and brand."

So what type of sponsorships could be pursued?

- *Media Sponsors to offer publicity support*
- *Sole Sponsor for the entire sponsorship responsibility*
- *Title Sponsor who only wants their name on event/product.*

Source: Independent Sector, 2003.

Despite recent growth in corporate sponsorship, in North America cultural organisations still only receive 12 per cent of the total amount corporations spend on sports sponsorship alone. Despite this small percentage the demand for sponsorship arrangements with major US corporations is so great that they receive on average of 500 sponsorship proposals a year. The reason for the popularity of sponsorship agreements with corporations is that 84% of Americans say that they are likely to switch their purchasing to a competing brand, if the company supports charitable causes (Cone, 2002). Because of the demand, cultural organisations that are considering corporate sponsorship arrangements must carefully analyse what they have to offer and what they wish to achieve.

Benefits for the Corporation

Specific benefits the cultural organisation may offer to a corporation would certainly include access to the organisation's audience. This would not only include programme advertising opportunities but also access using direct mailings. The corporate world is interested in reaching the audiences of cultural organisations because they consist of the highly sought-after cultural "creatives" marketing segment. This group of individuals are high income and wish to spend their money in ways that confirm their status. This makes them particularly attractive to companies that sell luxury and high technology products (Ray, 1997).

Of course, the corporation would want free tickets to use for corporate hospitality. They also may wish to use tickets as part of their benefit package for all employees. In order to promote the corporate name and image, the corporation will want to display its name on the organisation's marquee and programmes. And finally, the cultural organisation can also offer use of its venue and exhibits or performances for corporate events.

If the sponsorship is a long-term arrangement, the corporation may wish to tie its image more closely to the cultural organisation by actually having a seat on the board. It may also wish to enhance the relationship by inviting employees of the cultural organisation and the artists to visit the corporation's work-site. Such visits could include exhibits and/or performances. It may do so in a belief that the artistic creative energy will actually make the employees more creative or simply to enhance the corporation's image.

Benefits of Sponsorship for Corporations

- Access to the organisation's audience.
- Use of venue/performances or events.
- Tickets for employees.
- Marquee/programme advertising.
- Seats on the board.

- Visiting artists or exhibits to work-site.
- Brand differentiation.

Benefits for the Cultural Organisation

The cultural organisation must also determine what it wants to receive from the sponsorship arrangement. Much more than funding can be sought and any additional benefits should be closely tied into the organisation's marketing strategy. Just as the corporation can use the cultural organisation to enhance its image, so the organisation can "piggy-back" on the corporation's image. Choosing a corporation that is popular with a potential target market segment can help the cultural organisation to position the cultural product so that it benefits from the association in consumers' minds. And just as the corporation can benefit from access to the cultural organisation's audience, the opposite is also true. The organisation can gain access to the corporation's clients, as well as to the corporation's employees.

Even a long-term relationship probably will not gain the cultural organisation a seat on the corporation's board. However the organisation can gain immensely from the expertise that the corporate employees can offer. For instance, the corporation's marketing department may be able to assist in developing new promotional ideas. Likewise, the strategies planning department may be able to assist the cultural organisation in determining its long-range goals.

Benefits to the Cultural Organisation

- Funds for special projects.
- In-kind donations.
- Enhanced image.
- Positioning of product.
- Access to client/customer.
- Access to employees.
- Sharing of expertise in marketing and strategy.

Available Opening: Corporate Sponsor for the RSC

Before it was enough for corporate sponsors to have their name in the programme – but not any more! The Royal Shakespeare Company (RSC) does not just wait for corporate sponsors to come to them – they market!

Its website has posted information on the benefits available to new corporate sponsors:

> *"For our corporate partners, we can offer our high profile as one of the world's most recognised theatre companies, access to our loyal audiences and our unique entertaining facilities to assist you in achieving your commercial objectives – client hospitality, brand development or meeting social responsibility targets."*

The RSC spells out the benefits sponsorship can bring:

- *Exclusive entertaining opportunities around fantastic shows*
- *Access to a broad audience of many segments*
- *Flexible ticket packages*
- *Staff discounts*
- *Acknowledgement in all programmes for one year.*

Source: Royal Shakespeare Company, 2003.

Corporate Membership

The traditional arrangement for corporate sponsorship is for the corporation to provide funding in monetary or in-kind donation, in return for which the name of the corporation is prominently (or discreetly) displayed on posters and programmes. A new arrangement is to have corporations join as "members" of the cultural organisation. In this arrangement, the corporation moves from being a passive to an active partner in the relationship.

Membership agreements are negotiated contractual agreements with set benefits and a limited, but specified, life span, typically yearly and easily renewable. The fees charged to companies becoming corporate members provide a predictable source of income to the organisation (Boodle, 1997). In return, the cultural organisation provides the corporation with "value-added" benefits. These benefits include the ability to meet last-minute requests for tickets to popular events that the corporation needs to entertain clients. The cultural organisation can also arrange backstage tours and use of the venue for corporate events. For the corporation, membership also includes intangible benefits, such as access to those who create art and manage the organisation.

NEW SOURCES OF FUNDING

As cultural organisations struggle to replace declining funding from tax revenue, a number of new ideas are being tried. Many European cultural organisations are now trying an American idea, which is to create an *endowment fund* (Morris, 1999). The money raised is invested and only the proceeds used to fund operating expenses. Because individuals need to be persuaded to donate large sums to these funds, the marketing department is intimately involved in planning and running the endowment campaign.

To cut back on using tax money for funding the arts, some governments have established *lotteries*. These lotteries have become a very popular means of indirect taxation to support the arts. It has been noticed by some commentators, however, that lower income individuals are the main purchasers of lottery tickets, while high income individuals attend the arts. The result is that the high art forms are supported by lottery ticket purchases made by individuals who infrequently, or never, attend.

Another new source of income is *merchandising*. Some cultural organisations are even partnering with businesses which provide the expertise on how this can be done.

Yet another source of funding which has seen a resurgence of popularity is *employee workplace giving*. In the US, workplace donations for the arts were $14.6 million in 1997 (Underwood, 1999). In this type of scheme, the cultural organisation asks the corporation to solicit funds on its behalf. These donations are made through payroll deductions and the amount is forwarded to the cultural organisation. This idea can be coupled with donating reduced price tickets to events for those who contribute. In this way, the cultural organisation raises funds, while also encouraging attendance.

People Love Festivals

Film festivals are increasingly popular in Australia with record attendance numbers turning out to see difficult and demanding films. Does this mean that there is new growth in committed cinephiles? According to Melbourne director James Hewison, a crucial factor in the success of film festivals is that they are community events. It is important that the cinemas be close together along with nearby bars and cafés. They may come to enjoy the experience but also leave having experienced films they would never otherwise see.

Sources: Barber, 2003.

Collaborative Efforts

One response to diminishing funding support has been for cultural organisations to work collaboratively in mounting events. This growth in collaborative efforts has also been spurred because they are particularly attractive to funding bodies, which believe that it will cut costs while increasing creativity. The best reason for undertaking a collaborative effort with another cultural organisation or a corporate body is to accomplish something that cannot be accomplished alone.

For a partnership to be successful, the following questions need to be answered before the collaborative effort is launched:

- What is the motivation for embarking on the partnership?
- Are there any hidden agendas or self-interests that should be made clear?
- What resources and problems is each partner bringing to the partnership?
- How will communication take place?
- Who makes decisions?
- How will the decisions be implemented?
- How will the partnership know it has been successful?

And the Small Shall Gather Together: Connecticut Art Trail

How can 12 separate museums and historic sites work together to attract visitors? By publicising the common theme of American Impressionist Art. The museums and sites are all located within the same geographic area and are all associated with, or show, art created during the flowering of American Impressionism during the 1920s. In 1995, the Connecticut Art Trail was launched with the goal of attracting both local visitors and tourists to visit the museums while enjoying the scenic area.

The collaboration had been conceived at a meeting of museum directors as a way to increase visibility and attendance. With a small state grant to help cover start-up and marketing costs, the museums worked with a graphics firm to design a brochure that was distributed to hotels and welcome centres. A short video was also produced, which was sent to group tour operators. In addition, a public relations firm was hired to ensure that the idea received sufficient coverage in the news.

The initial result was over 35,000 written requests for the brochure from 47 US states and 12 foreign countries. Although it is difficult to determine how much of attendance was due to the campaign, during the first year there was an average attendance increase at the museums of 35 per cent and an additional 9 per cent in the second year. This result was achieved by pooling the resources of the cultural organisations involved. For only a total investment of $4,200 over three years, they received publicity they could not have generated on their own.

The programme is still going strong and the brochure can now be requested on the programme's own website of www.arttrail.org.

Source: Thurston, 1997; Connecticut Impressionist Art Trail, 2003.

IMPLICATIONS OF NON-PROFIT STATUS

Besides the continuing concern with funding, the fact that cultural organisations are non-profit has a negative impact on their managerial effectiveness. One of the negative impacts is that the absence of a profit motive makes it difficult for the cultural organisation to measure success. The classic goal of making a profit lets businesses know quickly whether they are successful. Even if the business states that its goal is to have satisfied customers, the attainment of this goal is measured by the level of revenue. After all, if customers were not satisfied, they would not buy the product.

Implications for Measuring Goals

Because earning a profit is not a goal for them, cultural organisations face a difficulty in determining what their goals and objectives are and whether they have been met. One common goal of a cultural organisation is to expose the public to the art form in the belief that such exposure enriches the community. This is a praiseworthy goal, but it is difficult to measure.

If the community does not support the art form, and therefore is not enriched, the cultural organisation may view the public, not the organisation, as responsible for the failure of the mission. In fact, for some cultural organisations, the absence of customers is accepted as a sign of success because it is seen as a consequence of maintaining high artistic standards. Indeed, the cultural organisation may believe that the majority of the public is too ignorant to appreciate the art form. This can be the unfortunate result when the source of revenue is separated from the customer, because there is less need for cultural organisations to incorporate the public's desires in their goals.

External Pressures

The reliance on other sources than revenue for funding also leaves the cultural organisation susceptible to political pressure and other external influences and trends. The organisation may be subject to pressure from a board of trustees, who are also major donors, to adhere to a manner of presenting art that has limited appeal to today's audience. Or the opposite pressure, to popularise the art to increase attendance in a way that the organisation feels is inappropriate, may come from the government. If the cultural organisation relies on fundraising, it can become hostage to the competing claims of special interest groups, which may keep the organisation from making changes it knows should be made.

Financial Implications

Non-profit status also has practical financial implications. Since there is no excess revenue, the organisation has limited means to motivate staff financially. This can result in employees who are unresponsive to customer needs, as additional attendance will not benefit them. Having small personnel budgets, cultural organisations often must rely on volunteers, which, while less expensive for the payroll, may cost considerably more in time and effort than managing paid employees. And the organisation's inability to pay executive salaries commensurate with business makes it more difficult to compete for top talent.

A last constraint that results from non-profit status is that it is difficult for cultural organisations to build up a cash reserve to pay for the ever-increasing cost of technology. If London's for-profit West End theatres are using expensive special effects, the theatre audience may expect the same from the local theatre, which cannot possibly afford to provide them. Even museums are facing this challenge, as visitors are no longer willing to view objects passively, but instead want to be involved by using the latest technology such as interactive computer screens.

Implications for Creativity

There has always been tension in cultural organisations between those creating art and those responsible for presenting art (Ní Bhrádaigh, 1997). In fact, this creative tension is sometimes necessary for art to happen. Those working in cultural organisations have always argued about the meaning and definition of art, and how art should be presented. For example, a cultural organisation may be torn internally over how it should present a performance, heated discussions might be held over the vision of the artistic director, there might be feuds in the orchestra over the repertoire which should be played, and the new playwright might be proclaimed a visionary by some and a failure by others. These tensions remained within the artistic and cultural family. Once a consensus was reached over what art to present, the public was expected to accept the decision. They might disagree and not attend but this was not considered a serious problem. This disconnection between the public and the product was possible because the cultural organisation was not reliant on the customer for revenue.

Instead, the cultural organisation relied on the government for funding. There was a well-established policy in most countries that, while the government should fund the arts, it should not be involved in decisions concerning the creation or presentation of art. Cultural organisations expected that they should receive the money with no questions asked and no advice given.

This traditional "arm's length" policy of funding is no longer as true. Now, when a cultural organisation accepts government funding, it is also faced with increased political pressure to be responsive to the public. This pressure comes from the government's belief that, if the taxpayers are providing the funding, cultural organisations have certain obligations to them, including ensuring that the art presented is of interest to the public. While cultural organisations would argue that the arts are of interest to everyone, it is also true that attendance at the high art forms has always been skewed toward higher-income and better-educated individuals. Now organisations must prove to funders that they not only welcome everyone but that they are taking active steps to encourage attendance from everyone.

EXCELLENCE *VERSUS* ACCESSIBILITY

If the cultural organisation wishes to be considered in the top tier of similar organisations, their organisational strategy will require additional funding to pay for star performers or exhibits. This necessity will then make the organisation even more dependent on, and answerable to, the government that provides the funding. The result can be tension over the issue of excellence *versus* accessibility. The artistic director or curator will be focused on providing a production or exhibit of the very highest artistic quality that may appeal only to those who have a sophisticated appreciation of the art. On the other hand, those responsible for procuring funding will want a performance or exhibit that will appeal to those who are currently not attending, to prove to the government that they have the support of the community.

Conflicts between the cultural organisation and the government over the issue of accessibility can also arise over whether the focus on the cultural organisation should be on traditional or new art forms. Many within the organisation may wish to remain faithful to a traditional form of the art that appeals to a limited number of people, while government funders may pressure the organisation to provide more accessible art. However if the organisation does present more contemporary or popular art that attracts new attenders, it may antagonise those currently loyal to the organisation.

What is a Social Entrepreneur?

"A social entrepreneur is someone who works in an entrepreneurial manner, but for public or social benefit, rather than to make money. Social entrepreneurs may work in ethical business, governmental or public bodies, quangos, or the voluntary and community sector.

While entrepreneurs in the business sector identify untapped commercial markets, and gather together the resources to break into those markets for profit, social entrepreneurs use the same skills to different effect. For social entrepreneurs, untapped markets are people or communities in need, who haven't been reached by other initiatives."

Source: School for Social Entrepreneurs, 2003.

SOCIAL ENTREPRENEURSHIP

As cultural organisations struggle to survive in the new competitive climate with increasingly limited resources, a new model has been evolving. Social entrepreneurship is characterised by using the same creative, fast-paced, market-responsive, and risk-taking qualities that are common among new start-up companies (Hirschfield, 1999). The difference is that these qualities are used in service of a non-profit goal rather than to produce a for-profit good or service. This new type of organisation exhibits a blurring of the traditional boundaries between non-profit and for-profit.

The social entrepreneur uses the same model as used by the high-tech start-up. Rather than assume the public is interested in the cultural product that the social entrepreneurs want to produce, they spend considerable time researching the market and potential customers before they begin to offer the product.

The social entrepreneur considers initial fund-raising in the same terms as raising venture capital. They want funding sources that are long-term and that are willing to play a role in establishing the organisation through resources and contacts, not just by giving money. In response, there has been a growth in entrepreneurial foundations that are interested in giving the long-term support needed by social entrepreneurs.

Another of the unique characteristics of social entrepreneurs is their team approach to solving problems. This is in contrast to the departmental approach of most traditional cultural organisations, where the department that produces the cultural product is carefully protected from the other departments. Along with this team approach is an emphasis on accountability. It is expected that the organisation will be successful in meeting its goals and the recurring deficits that are the mark of most traditional cultural organisations are not acceptable. The organisation started by social entrepreneurs is very focused on a specific, and even time-limited, cultural need rather than having the more traditional mission of improving society.

Unique Features of Social Entrepreneur Organisations

- Preliminary market research.
- Reliance on partnerships with long-term funding sources.
- Team/network oriented.
- Accountability for outcomes.
- Focus on what is best for customer/public.
- Financially self-sufficient.
- Niche-oriented.

Hugo House: A Social Entrepreneurial Success

The Richard Hugo House (named after a local poet) opened in 1997 in an old converted Victorian house in Seattle. The House was founded as an entrepreneurial start-up to provide a place that would be a welcoming community for local writers and community members interested in writing.

A year of preliminary market research and community planning went into the project. Since its opening, over 10,000 people have come to Hugo House for classes, workshops, events, performances, meetings or just to visit. Why has it been a success? According to the founders, among the essential elements for success were passionate and business-savvy founders with a clear mission and vision that meet a real community need.

Sources: Hirschfied, 1999; Richard Hugo House, 2004.

In summary, cultural organisations are not able to raise all their needed revenue directly from customers. However, they still must understand the three basic approaches to pricing, which are cost, competition and prestige and the role price plays as in the attendance decision. They then will be less dependent on fundraising, although alternative means of raising funds will always be important sources of revenue for cultural organisations.

Pricing Worksheet

Use this checklist to help determine the effect of raising ticket prices. The more 'yes' answers the more freedom to raise prices.

Question	Yes	No	?
Do our customers seem to be unaware of price increases?			
Is our customer base expanding?			
Does our status or reputation increase our value?			
Are we in an established market rather than a new market?			
Do we have many customers who attend infrequently rather than a smaller number of repeat customers?			
Do we have full houses instead of lots of empty seats?			
Do our customers spend money on other similar products?			

These questions can help you to determine a pricing strategy:

1. What are our expenses?

    _____

    _____

2. What other sources of revenue besides ticket sales do we have?

    _____

    _____

3. What do our competitors charge?

    _____

    _____

4. What is the price range our customers expect?

    _____

    _____

5. How can differential pricing be used to increase revenue from existing customers?

    _____

    _____

6. How can differential pricing be used to attract new customers?

    _____

    _____

7. How can pricing be used as a sales incentive?

    _____

    _____

References

Barer, Lynden (2003) "Finding a Niche Between Purity and Popularity" in *The Australian* August 13.

Boodle, C. (1997) "Making Friends with Influence", in *Museums Journal*, December.

Cone Corporate Citizenship Study (2002) online at coneinc.com/pages/research.

Connecticut Impressionist Art Trail (2003) online at www.arttrail.org.

Field, K.M. (1999) "Winning Strategies for Corporate Sponsorships" in *Arts Reach*, August.

Hirschfield, Laura (1999) "Richard Hugo House: A Study in Social Entrepreneurship", in *Lessons Learned: Case Studies*, National Endowment for the Arts, online at: www.arts.endow.gov/pub/Lessons.

Hogwood, Christopher (1977) *Music At Court*, The Folio Society, London.

Independent Sector: The Resource Center for Effective Corporate-Nonprofit Partnerships (2003) online at independentsector.org/mission_market/partnerships.

Jensen, Joli (2002) *Is Art Good for Us?: Beliefs about High Culture in American Life*, Rowman & Littlefield Publishers, Inc.

Moloney, Mary (2003) "Helping out a Friend in Need" in *The Irish Times*, Sept. 8.

Morris, Jane (1999) "Want to be Well-endowed?", in *International Arts Manager*, December/January.

Ní Bhrádaigh, E. (1997) "Arts Marketing: A Review of Research and Issues", in *From Maestro to Manager: Critical Issues in Arts & Culture Management*, Oak Tree Press.

Ray, P.H. (1997) "The Emerging Culture", in *American Demographics*, February.

Richard Hugo House (2004) online at www.hugohouse.org/about.

Royal Shakespeare Company, Corporate Support (2003) online at: www.rsc.org.uk/supportthersc/389.asp.

San Diego Opera (2004) "Frequently Asked Questions" online at www.sdopera.net.

Scher, V. (2002) "Arts 'Salesman' Follows Own Advice: Make 'em Subscribe" *San Diego Union Tribune*, April 21.

School for Social Entrepreneurs (2003) online at www.sse.org.uk/network/learning/what_is_social_entrepreneur.

The Washington Times (2002) "Analysis: Saving Public Arts Funding" online at washingtontimes.com/upi-breaking/20031117-072921-1489r.htm. Nov 23.

Thurston, Tony (1997) "Connecticut Art Trail", in *Arts Reach*, September.

Underwood, Consuelo (1999) "Workplace Giving: A Source for Arts Support", in *Lessons Learned: Case Studies*, National Endowment for the Arts, online at: www.arts.endow.gov/pub/Lessons.

Chapter Ten

THE PROMOTION MIX

Often when people are asked to define marketing, they will describe the promotion of a product. But the promotion of a product to consumers is actually the final step in the strategic marketing process, not the first. Before promotion can be done, the cultural organisation must first understand the external societal environment and how it affects the market for their product. It must research its target audience segment to discover the benefits that it desires. It must also understand how to package its product to include the desired benefits, price it correctly and find the right venue in which to distribute. Only then is the organisation ready to put together a promotional campaign. Now it knows to whom it is speaking and what needs to be said. With this knowledge, the cultural organisation can design a message that will be understandable and appealing to its target market segment.

Once the message is created, the cultural organisation then will decide how it should be communicated. The choices of method are advertising, sales incentives, personal selling, public relations and direct marketing. The current trend is to use integrated marketing communications (IMC), where the cultural organisation uses more than one promotional method to deliver the same message to increase its likelihood of being heard.

THE MESSAGE

Cultural organisations understand that they need to communicate a message about their product to the public. Since most organisations assumed that everyone would be interested in their art form, they have traditionally used advertising to broadcast a general marketing message that only provided information on the cultural product's features, such as programming and artists. They assumed that consumers were already motivated to attend and understood the benefits they would receive. This type of promotional message communicates to consumers' intellect but not to their emotions.

However benefits, such as socialisation and entertainment, are often emotional in nature. Consumers respond both intellectually and emotionally to a promotional message and, therefore, the message should address both. Most of the marketing promotion done by cultural organisations has been designed to make culture enthusiasts intellectually aware of the current arts programming they are offering. The assumption is that the benefits associated with the product, whether dance, theatre or classical music, are already understood. If cultural organisations are marketing to culture consumers who have limited or no knowledge of the product class or form, marketing of specific features will have little meaning and, therefore, little ability to motivate them to attend.

What a Difference a Few Words Can Make!

The Virginia Chorale needed an advertisement for their fundraising campaign. When first designed the headline read:

   "Yes! I Will Help to Keep the Chorale Singing".

A very noble sentiment and hopefully people would respond unselfishly. But after a makeover, the new headline read:

   "Yes! Count me in! Let me Help! I Want to be Part of the Excitement!

Now the target market understands that, besides being altruistic if they give money, they will also benefit directly by being part of something exciting.

Source: Zorn, 2001.

DIFFUSION OF INNOVATION

Consumers vary in their willingness to try new products (Rogers, 1962). When introducing a new cultural product to an established audience, or attracting a new audience to an existing product, it is important for the cultural organisation to understand the difficulty inherent in motivating individuals to try something new, as many people are averse to taking risks. When promoting a new cultural product, the cultural organisation will need a different message depending on whether the individual is risk-averse or adventurous.

Innovators

The theory of the diffusion of innovation groups the public by their willingness to try new products. Innovators, who make up only 2.5 per cent of the total population, are those who are willing to be the first to try a product. Innovators seek stimulation and are attracted to such events as opening nights, new productions and cutting-edge art. They have enough money that they can afford to take the risk of trying the unfamiliar. Because Innovators are influential and well connected, if they like what they have experienced, they will spread the word to others, who will then be interested in attending.

Diffusion of Innovation Theory

Type	%	Description
Innovator	2.5%	Younger. Financially stable and well educated.
Early Adopter	13.5%	Similar but larger group of trend setters. Knowledgeable about art form.
Early Majority	34%	Follow trendsetters. Middle class.
Late Majority	34%	Follow Early Majority. Older and more conservative than Early Majority.
Laggards	13.5%	Possibilities but difficult to reach and motivate.
Non-adopters	2.5%	Find culture threatening. Attempt to neutralise hostility.

Early Adopters

Those consumers who follow the example of the Innovators are the Early Adopters. Early Adopters are trendsetters, who are similar demographically to the Innovators but are not as well connected or knowledgeable and, therefore, are less likely to take risks. They will attend because they have heard that the exhibit or performance is the one that everyone considered "in the know" must see. It is crucial that this group be satisfied with the cultural event or else acceptance of the product will not move on to the larger groups of Early Majority and Late Majority consumers.

Early and Late Majority

The Early and Late Majority groups of consumers are mostly from the middle-class and follow the advice of other more influential groups when making decisions. The Early Majority purchase first and the Late Majority take the lead from them.

The Early Majority are not going to take the risk of purchasing anything unknown but will take their lead from the media. If they see that the Early Adopters have made a hit of a performance or exhibit, they will then also attend. The Early Majority are distinguished from the Late Majority by being younger and wealthier.

The Late Majority trusts the word of their friends and neighbours. Only if they have had an enjoyable experience will the Late Majority attend. The cultural product is now reaching the mass market. Of course, at this point the Innovators and Early Adopters would no longer be interested in attending.

Laggards and Non-Adopters

The Laggards are those consumers who have no interest in new experiences. In fact, they might find new experiences upsetting, rather than exciting. Laggards lack the confidence to walk into a theatre or museum because they fear they will not know what is going on and might possibly be ridiculed. In reality, it is very difficult for a cultural organisation to motivate them to attend. They can probably be reached only by bringing the cultural product to a venue in which they are comfortable.

The Non-Adopter is not only uninterested, but is actually hostile to culture because their sense of self and value system is threatened by any experience with which they are uncomfortable. With this group, the most that the cultural organisation can hope to accomplish is to try to neutralise the hostility. It is very important to not communicate an image of élitism to Non-Adopters, which would simply antagonise them even more.

Need Volunteers? Ask For Help Online!

Websites are a great place to put out the word on volunteer opportunities. For example, the Niagara Volunteer Connection website allows potential volunteers to find organisations that need their skill. Listed are 1,140 available opportunities needing a total of 5,920 individuals. Users can search for either a specific organisation or they can search by skill. To ensure the best match, volunteer opportunities can also be searched for by geographic area and the day/time of the need. Opportunities available range from:

- *Niagara Symphony needs people to help sell CD, books and other items during intermission*
- *Welland Historical Museum needs a floor painter*
- *The Grimsby Public Art Gallery needs a tour guide.*

Get your needs on a database and get some help!

Source: Information Niagara, 2004.

Promotional Messages & Diffusion of Innovation

The cultural organisation must consider whether its targeted market segment is likely to be attracted to new products or would rather wait. For instance, when the organisation plans new performance programming or a new exhibit, it may need to communicate a different message to different acceptance types during each stage of the cultural product life cycle. When the product is new, the message should be targeted directly at those selected individuals who are Innovators. Then advertising for later performances should be aimed at the Early Adopters. As this group wants to feel exclusive and knowledgeable, the advertising message should communicate that this new, exciting experience is being produced for the enjoyment of people such as themselves.

Further into the run of the performance or exhibit, a more broadly based message should be communicated to the Early Majority using reviews and comments made by the Early Adopters. And, finally, in the last stage of the advertising campaign, the event can be promoted to the Late Majority as "the show that your neighbour has seen and loved".

Message Contents

The message content is what needs to be said to a specific target market segment to motivate them to buy. The cultural organisation may have more than one message for the same art product or event. In fact, because the benefits desired will vary between groups, it will almost always have to do so.

Not all organisations use a marketing message. If the organisation is a well-known brand whose benefits are widely recognised, it might not need a message. The first page of the New York Metropolitan Opera website only provides a listing of subjects such as "Season Schedule", "Join the Met Family" and "Opera Broadcasts". The Met assumes that the consumer is already motivated to obtain more information (Metropolitan, 2004).

By contrast, a visit to the first page of the website for New York City Opera will tell the consumer that City Opera's founding mission is to "make opera matter". A bit of a vague message, but at least a message that encourages the consumer to find out how City Opera makes opera matter. A click on "Who is NYCO?" answers the question by explaining that the benefits that attenders will receive are innovative opera with a focus on American productions, and ticket prices that are affordable (New York City Opera, 2004).

An example of a more powerful message regarding the benefits of attending opera is the Opera Carolina website (Opera Carolina, 2004). Because it is not a well-known brand name, it uses emotion to attract attention. Its first page says "Power. Love. Jealousy. Madness. Better get a good seat." These words are at the top of the page on a deep red background. Below are the details on programming and ticket purchase. The message clearly states that the culture consumer can attend for emotional reasons and not because they know anything about opera. The message communicates that anyone who finds power, love, jealousy and madness exciting will enjoy opera.

A Message to Demystify

The Cincinnati Symphony Orchestra, as part of a branding campaign, found that people were not attending because they thought that enjoying the music would take some type of specialized knowledge. So the orchestra chose as its marketing message: "Bring Your Emotions".

To demystify and personalize the orchestra further, advertisements showed close-ups of Paavo Järvi conducting with passion and energy. And to show that people who enjoy classical music are not all boring, the ads also informed readers that Paavo is an ex-heavy metal drummer!

Sources: Stone, 2001.

PROMOTION TASKS

Product promotion can be thought of as performing three different tasks: informative, persuasive, and reminder.

Informative promotion only informs the consumer of the product features. This is a necessary part of the promotional message, which alone is not enough to persuade new audiences to attend. The informative task is necessary when a new cultural product is being introduced. The opening of a new gallery with visual art by an unknown artist will require that information be provided to the public both about the venue and the artist.

Persuasive promotion seeks to encourage consumers with the benefits of attending. This task is necessary when aiming a message at culture consumers who may be unfamiliar with the cultural product. The purpose of the message is to present both facts about the product and the reason it should be consumed.

Reminder promotion focuses on reminding consumers of when and where the product is available. This promotion is most useful with culture enthusiasts. They are already familiar with and desire the product's features and benefits. The promotional material now just needs to inform them of programme, date and time.

When attracting cultural consumers, persuasive promotion is needed. However, the same organisation could use reminder promotion to its cultural enthusiasts who already attend the organisation or attend a competing organisation. In fact, the cultural enthusiast might find the persuasive message promotion with its emphasis of other benefits than artistic quality overly aggressive.

PROMOTION METHODS

Now that the cultural organisation has a message, it must decide what method it will use to communicate its message to the target market segment. The choices are advertising, sales incentives, personal selling, public relations and direct marketing. The ideal is to use as many of the methods as possible to communicate the message so there is the best chance of getting heard.

Advertising

Advertising is the word that most people immediately associate with promotion. Often the words are used interchangeably, but they are not the same as advertising is only one means of promotion. Advertising is not new – messages for the upcoming bouts of popular gladiators have been found on the walls of Pompeii. Modern advertising campaigns date from the birth of the technological, radio and television, to deliver advertisements to a mass group of people.

Advertising may be only one of the methods that can be used to promote a product, but it is probably the most noticeable. This is because advertising, defined as non-personal communication, is widely broadcast. The fact that is widely broadcast is both its strength and also its weakness. It is advertising's strength because its wide dissemination means it will be seen by many people. The weakness results from the fact that it must compete for attention with all the other advertisements trying to do the same. People have become so deluged with advertised messages that they have "tuned out".

Advertising is usually associated with the broadcast mediums of TV and radio. Advertising professionals are often needed to design this type of broadcast advertising campaign because they have the needed expertise. Small cultural organisations rarely have the money to put into this type of advertising promotion. However there are also less expensive means that cultural organisations can use such as print advertising through newspapers, magazines, billboards, posters/flyers and brochures. In designing print advertisements, three elements are essential for success:

- The marketing message must be crafted into a memorable word or phrase.
- The design must be creative and appealing to the target market segment.
- The necessary factual information, such as when, where and what, must be provided.

Advertising seems to be everywhere, from the back of ticket stubs to the seat backs in public buses (and toilets). Advertisements can even be found on video screens in elevators, small placards mounted on gasoline pumps and even in light on floors and walls using floodlights. However, despite its pervasiveness, advertising is not the most common form of promotion. In fact the percentage of all promotional dollars spent on advertising in the US is declining (Cappo, 2003).

What Information Should Your Ad Provide?
Facts, Benefits and a Call to Action!

After the creative work on your ad has been done and it's looking great, take another look at it through the eyes of someone in your target market segment. Be sure it answers the following questions – and that it doesn't take more than five to ten seconds to do so!

> *What is this about?*
>
> *Why should I care?*
>
> *What am I supposed to do?*

Unfortunately, after getting the reader hooked, some organisations hide in the bottom of their ad the contact information. If the needed information is too hard to find, the reader is on to the next ad and you have lost a potential customer.

Source: Ruddle, 2000.

Sales Incentives

An area of promotion that is growing in favour among profit businesses is sales incentives. Sales incentives are a promotion method that is used to stimulate product trial among non-purchasers and to increase demand or purchase frequency among current customers. While advertising uses a marketing message to provide facts about the product and the benefits that will result from its consumption, sales incentives communicate a marketing message along with an incentive that provides a very specific motivation for buying right now.

Sales incentives are of growing importance in the field of promotion for three reasons:

- They can be carefully targeted to encourage attendance by specific market segments or for a specific art event.
- They can be relatively inexpensive compared with advertising.
- They allow the organisation to gather demographic and other information.

Creativity is the key to a successful sales incentive promotion. Common sales incentives that can be used include discounts, coupons, premiums, contests and samples. However, there are many more types used by profit businesses that could be adapted for use by cultural organisations.

Discounts are when a temporary price reduction is used. The reduction might be given to help fill seats when demand is low or to introduce a new product. Everyone loves the sense of getting a good deal. Even people who have large incomes like to feel that they are smart consumers.

Discounts also add excitement to the purchase process by giving a compelling reason to "buy now" (Hine, 2002). An example of a discount would be 25% off the purchase price of a second ticket for a limited time period. Such a discount can be planned and promoted or it can be instituted at the last moment for events that are selling slowly. Or a discount might be used to encourage sales for a less popular or new arts event by offering tickets at a discount when the consumer purchases a full price ticket to a more popular show.

Other ideas include having seasonal discounts for periods of time when attendance is slow, such as during the holidays. Discounted gift certificates might be sold as a Christmas special. Tourists might be targeted with discounted prices during the summer. Group discounts can be offered to clubs, service organisations or churches as a means to encourage attendance.

Coupons are similar to discounts but are usually in print form and target a specific product rather than time period. Coupons are usually used for the consumer goods market but there is no reason why they cannot be adapted for arts promotion.

A coupon offering two-for-one tickets could be sent to subscribers on their birthday. Or coupons could be included with all new single ticket purchases to encourage a return visit. If the coupon is not used, nothing is lost by the organisation but a small printing cost. If it is used, it will fill a seat that might have gone empty otherwise.

Cross-promotions are collaboration between two or more organisations. The idea is to encourage the customers of one business to patronise another related business. This could be a collaboration between two cultural organisations where one ticket purchase will allow entry to both venues. The price is usually less than it would be if the tickets were purchased separately.

But cross-promotions can also be used between cultural organisations and profit businesses. A ticket might include both the price of the ticket and the cost of dessert at a local restaurant. For those travelling to the event from out of town, the collaboration might be offering a package that includes the ticket and hotel stay.

Everyone Loves the Nutcracker at Christmas!

The Nutcracker Ballet is a Christmas holiday favourite that is popular year after year. Rather than just complain that it's Nutcracker time again, the Pennsylvania Ballet uses sales incentives to increase the audience for the Nutcracker even more. Some ideas they have instituted include:

- *For a discounted price, families can have their picture taken with the Mouse King in front of the Christmas tree.*

- *A cross-promotional package with a local hotel that includes a one night stay, tickets to the performance and breakfast the next morning.*

- *A contest "Nutty for the Nutcracker" with a prize of four free tickets, a Nutcracker fun pack and a free backstage tour.*

- *As a special premium, some performances include a free Family Day event featuring entertainment, games and craft activities.*

Source: Pennsylvania Ballet, 2003.

Premiums are gifts that are given free or at a very low cost to ticket purchasers. They are usually targeted at a specific group or for a specific event. Of course, cost is an issue. An organisation can help to defray the cost of the premium by using something they already have or by having the gift donated to the organisation. For example, a choral group might provide a free copy of its CD for all new subscription ticket purchasers. The cost of each additional CD to the organisation is low. New ticket purchasers are unfamiliar with the group's music and are therefore unlikely to buy the CD on their own. Meanwhile, the organisation sells additional tickets based on the promotion and the consumer will hopefully enjoy the CD and return for another performance. Another idea for a premium might be copies of posters that are paid for by a local business, which would then receive free publicity.

Contests are another way to encourage sales, while adding a bit of excitement to the purchase process. They are also an excellent method of collecting consumer data. The easiest is simply to have a drawing by asking people when purchasing their tickets to provide their business card or fill in an entry blank. The purpose of this type of contest is to attract entries from as many people as possible as a means of gathering names and demographic data. Asking for business cards works well. It is simple for the customer and the organisation can gather additional information such as employer and email address. The address and email is necessary, of course, so that the winner can be notified. Because of privacy issues, the entry form can include a box that can be checked requesting that the customer not be added to your email list.

The prize for the drawing can be for anything from a free mug to a free season ticket. Different audience segments can be encouraged to complete a form by changing the prize to something that will be of special interest. To keep costs down, the prize can be an experience rather than a product. Culture consumers want to be involved rather than passive, so a prize such as the opportunity to meet the actors or to 'guest' conduct the orchestra can be very attractive. Having lunch with the conductor where they can discuss upcoming programming can be very appealing to culture enthusiasts. Because these are very exciting prizes, entry to the contest can be restricted to those who purchase a certain level of tickets.

Contests can also be used as a method of conducting quick and easy research on the targeted group. On the entry form it might ask a simple question such as "Would you attend a concert of 20th century music?" Or "Which of the following plays would you be interested in seeing?". The results will not be statistically valid, but it is always a good idea to get consumer preference information when possible.

Samples are common sales incentives for consumer products such as toiletries and food. Using sampling involves giving away a bit of the product in the hopes that the consumer will be so impressed they will continue to purchase. It is a common experience to receive a free sample-size tube of toothpaste or to be offered a taste of a dessert at the grocers. If the consumer likes the product, they may purchase it again.

Samples can also be used by arts organisations. It is very difficult to attract attendance if the cultural organisation's targeted market segment is totally unfamiliar with the art product. Such a group will ignore the organisation's advertisements, if they notice them at all. The only means of familiarising them with the product may be to give them a sample, which will mean bringing the art to the targeted group. This is essentially what arts organisations are doing when they bring music or art to schoolchildren. Such sampling can also be targeted at adults by bringing a bit of the music, play or visual art where the target market is located such as places of employment, churches or other leisure venues such as restaurants.

Personal Selling

Personal selling is informing the consumers of the benefits of the product one at a time. The traditional means of personal selling is the salesman going door-to-door, which, of course, is not how arts are sold. However, personal selling is not just the job of a professional salesperson. Personal selling can be done by every member of the organisation, using every opportunity to inform each member of the public with whom they come into contact about the benefits the organisation provides.

For example, ticket sellers, when they sell a ticket for one performance should recommend another that might be of interest. Personal selling is for all members of the organisation – even the ushers. Of course, to be able to sell, the people in the organisation must be familiar with the product and be able to communicate its benefits to anyone with whom they may come into contact.

Public Relations

Broadly defined, public relations is about maintaining a favourable public image. It is a necessary tool when countering negative information about the organisation that may appear in the news media. While this is an important function of public relations, it is not how it is usually used by cultural organisations. They tend to focus more on the publicity component of public relations. Publicity is the creation of positive information on the organisation that is provided to the news media. The purpose of the publicity is to then generate positive coverage in the news media that will then be read by the public who will hopefully be motivated to attend. The principal tools are news releases, press conferences, photographs and feature articles.

For an organisation to use publicity effectively, it must have a good working relationship with the local media. Newspapers, radio stations and magazines work on tight time schedules and with specific production guidelines. If the news release or feature article is timely, in the correct format and aimed at the media's target audience, it has a much greater chance of being published.

In addition, it must be interesting. Newspapers, radio and other media are businesses that live or die by who is reading, listening or watching. These businesses will use your contribution, not to help you sell tickets, but because the information you have provided will be of interest to their audience.

Once you have decided on an appropriate media vehicle for your publicity, and established a relationship with them, then you need to write a press release or article or provide a photograph that will be used.

Getting Your News Noticed or How to Stand out from the Crowd

Newspapers, magazines, TV and radio all receive more press releases than they can handle. When you write, ask yourself these questions to help you get your publicity noticed:

- *Is your news unusual or unique?*
- *Does it have a local connection?*
- *How are people touched, involved, entertained or concerned?*
- *Which people and how many?*
- *Are children or animals involved?*
- *Does your story tie into another story that's hot right now?*
- *Will your story help people solve a problem?*

Source: Peithman and Offen, 1999.

Direct Marketing

Direct marketing serves two purposes. It promotes the product to a specific market segment by asking for immediate feedback through purchase or through a request for more information. And, secondly, it is used to maintain a database on the targeted customers so that future communications will be more focused on meeting the market segment needs. Direct marketing can be done via mail, phone or computer. Cultural organisations have relied on the phone and mail, but more are becoming sophisticated users of direct marketing using computer databases and email.

This makes sense as the average arts attender is well-educated and in a professional occupation. Being online is a routine part of their lives. The same is true of younger potential audience members. The use of the Internet has expanded so rapidly that, in 2002, 66% of all Americans were online, 55% of these at home and 30% online at work (Harris, 2002). And the most frequent activity for adults when online was checking their email.

Oh My, How You've Grown! Or the Web is Now Everywhere

Think that the use of the Internet is limited to certain countries? Wrong! And good news for cultural organisations is that the most popular use of search engines is to look for subjects dealing with entertainment. Here's some interesting numbers on Internet use:

- *544.2 million users worldwide or 1/12 of the world's population.*
- *147,344,723 separate websites as counted by hosts.*
- *60% of Internet users are from non-English speaking countries.*
- *48% of school children in India access the web at cyber cafés.*
- *37.5 million Chinese citizens use the web.*

Sources: CyberAtlas, 2004.

Creating Websites

Cultural organisations are quickly learning that websites are a necessary tool to provide information to the public on the features and benefits of their cultural product. They are now also learning that websites have other uses. A well designed website can communicate to the public the brand image of the organisation and the art form itself. Using video and music the public can view the dancing, see the art, and hear the music without setting foot into the venue.

Most people who access websites are doing so to find specific information. Although it is important to provide programme, location and contact facts that can be obtained with as few clicks as possible, the website is more than just an online brochure. The website can provide a direct connection to build a relationship between the consumer and the cultural organisation.

Besides providing information, the website can support direct purchase of tickets. Even if the organisation does not have the means to sell tickets online, there are other ways of getting a direct connection with website users. The organisation can build into the website a means for requesting more information. This information could then be sent in print form or via email. The website can also have a feature where users can send specific questions via email, which will receive a personal response. Once the cultural organisation knows what type of information people need, it can build a "Frequently Asked Questions" section into the website.

Email Clubs

The website can also be used to target specific market segments with specific types of information using email. There are basically three types of email. The first two are personal and commercial. Personal email is sent between two or more people known to each other. Commercial email, better known as the hated *spam*, is sent to millions, often using randomly created email addresses in the hopes it will get through. Spam now accounts for over half of all email sent and deservedly has a bad reputation. However, effective marketing programmes do not "blast" emails to everyone but instead focus on specific groups that have already requested information.

This is a third type of email called "opt-in". This email is a targeted list that is joined by request. When a customer of an arts organisation joins an email list, a marketing transaction is taking place. The customer is giving up a bit of their privacy in return for information of value to them (Carr, 2003). Therefore, email marketing should always be useful to the recipient. Having an email "club" can create this type of opt-in mailing list. The organisation should give the customer a chance to ask for specific types of information. When these requested emails are then received, they are not treated as spam but instead read.

The email club can be used to provide information on upcoming programming, special promotion offers, and special events. To reward the consumer for signing up, a special gift might be given. The Royal Opera offers email and mobile phone updates on productions, booking information and special offers. People who sign up can receive and download ring tones and also enter competitions (Royal Opera, 2004).

When sending out direct email to targets that request information, it is important that the information be personalised and customised. Most email is read quickly so the organisation must get to the point quickly (Roman and Maas, 2003). For example, the reason for the email message must be right at the beginning. Customising the subject line is also very important. The subject line of an email is the envelope the message comes in and must identify the sender. In addition, if the subject line is not interesting, the email might not be opened. For example, if the offer is geared toward families, or the email contains information on a pricing deal, it should say so in the subject line.

The organisation cannot send the emails if it does not have the addresses, so it is very important to use every means possible to collect this information. Some ideas are:

- Guest books or customer registration forms on the website.
- Including a line for email addresses on ticket order forms.
- Contests and promotions.
- Collecting at the box office.
- Lobby sign up sheets.
- Inserts in programmes.

When gathering email addresses, the cultural organisation should offer the customer signing up the ability to control the type and amount of information that is received. No one has time to read information in which they have no interest.

Developing a Personal Relationship

Using technology, vast quantities of information can be gathered on current and potential customers. Databases allow this information about what art events consumers actually purchase to be collected, and processed. This information on the consumers' demographics and consumer behaviour can assist the marketing department in segmenting their audience.

Even Churches Now Use Websites and Email to Market

The Christian Cultural Center in Brooklyn, New York wants to welcome new members to its church. So it has volunteers asking anyone entering who is new to the church to fill in a short card with contact information. The cards serve two purposes. Before the service begins, the pastor welcomes the visitors by name plus, the email allows for future follow-up contact. To maintain the relationship, on the church website, anyone can request counselling, volunteer their services or give a prayer or praise report – completely online.

Source: Christian Cultural Center, 2004.

The mission for cultural organisations may continue to be to reach the largest number of individuals with their cultural product. There remains the fact that their product may be of deep interest to enthusiasts who make up only a percentage of the population. Using databases, the cultural organisation can separate these individuals and use fewer resources to get their message across. The organisation's marketing strategy needs to differentiate between the more dedicated enthusiasts and groups of culture consumers. Separate direct marketing messages can focus on each group's interests.

It may be even more effective to further sub-divide these groups into very small and specialised segments that can be targeted for exactly the programmes or events they wish to attend. The cultural organisation can then use databases to email target culture consumers with a message that contains information on the emotional benefits that they desire.

Databases help to make this possible and, if used well, they can personalise the message so that a relationship is established between the cultural organisation and the audience. This personal relationship will stress not only the cultural product that they enjoy, but also how they can become involved with the organisation. For the cultural enthusiast, the association with the values of the cultural organisation is critical. The use of email and database programmes brings a new opportunity for even small organisations to bring a personal touch to all communication and outreach.

A further use of a website is to establish a dialogue between the public and the cultural organisation using chat rooms. The website can be used to solicit information on both the public's reactions to current programming and also their preference for future events.

The Audience is No Longer Silent

Part of the Royal Court Theatre's mission is to be a "force for addressing the problems and possibilities of our time". This cannot be done in isolation, so the website is used to build a community among its theatregoers. The website user can click on "Interact", which will bring them to either "chat" or "discuss". These features allow the public to interact directly with the playwright and other theatre attenders to debate and discuss questions they wish to pose.

Or you can "Yak with Yara" online at the Toronto Symphony's website. The web page site is described as: "Finally, a place where music lovers can discuss and voice their opinions on the world of music." After registration, you can join an online community that enjoys giving their views.

Source: Royal Court Theatre, 2004; Toronto Symphony Orchestra, 2004.

In summary, a promotional message that merely provides programme details is not an effective use of resources. It is a type of "non-marketing" message that feels comfortable to many who work in cultural organisations because it does not appear to "sell". This type of message assumes that the consumer already knows why they should attend, and so does not provide information on the benefits received by attending. However it is this information on specific benefits that motivates new culture consumers. Only through understanding all the benefits the product provides can the cultural organisation design an effective promotional message.

Promotion Plan Worksheet

First make sure you know your message and target.

Our marketing message is:

_____

_____

Our target market is:

_____

_____

Now design an integrated marketing communication plan.

Method	Who?	Cost?	Proposed Idea
Advertising (print, broadcast, flyer, brochure)			
Public relations (press releases, feature articles, photographs)			
Personal selling (staff training, box office workshops)			
Sales incentives (coupons, discounts, premiums, cross-promotions)			
Direct marketing (direct mail, email marketing)			

References

Cappo. J. (2003) *The Future of Advertising: New Media, New Clients, New Consumers*, McGraw Hill.

Carr, E. (2003) *Wired for Culture: How Email is Revolutionizing Arts Marketing*, Patron Publishing.

Christian Cultural Center (2004) online at www.clc.org.

CyberAtlas Staff (2004) *The Big Picture* online at www.Cyberatlas.internet.com/big_picture.

Harris Interactive (2002) "Internet Penetration at 66% of Adults (137 Million) Nationwide Internet Penetration at 66% of Adults (137 Million) Nationwide" online at www.harrisinteractive.com/harris_poll.

Hine, T. (2002) *I Want that! How we all Became Shoppers: A Cultural History*, Perennial.

Information Niagara (2004) online at niagara.cioc.ca/volunteer.

Metropolitan Opera (2004) online at www.methopera.org.

New York City Opera (2004) online at www.nycopera.com.

Opera Carolina (2004) online at www.operacarolina.org.

Peithman, S. and Offen, N. (1999) *Stage Directions Guide to Publicity*, Heinemann.

Pennsylvania Ballet (2003) Press Release: "CBS3 and Pennsylvania Ballet Present 35th Anniversary of Annual Holiday Spectacular The Nutcracker" online at www.paballet.org.

Rogers, E. (1962) *Diffusion of Innovations*, The Free Press.

Roman, K. and Maas, J. with Nisenholtz, M. (2003) *How to Advertise*, Thomas Dunne Books.

Royal Court Theatre (2004) "Interact" online at royalcourttheatre.com/interact

Royal Opera (2004) "Email and mobile phone updates" online at www.info.royaloperahouse.org/updates.

Ruddle, H. (2000) "It Doesn't Take Much to Make a Good Ad into a Highly Effective Ad" *Arts Reach*, March.

Stone, M. (2001) "The Cincinnati Symphony Sees Results from Their Branding and Image Upgrade Campaign" *Arts Reach*, November.

Toronto Symphony Orchestra (2004) "Yak with Yara" online at www.tso.ca/cgi-bin/ubbcgi/Ultimate.cgi.

Zorn, J. (2001) "Yes! It's Working!: Arts Reach Subscribers Take Ad Makeovers to Heart" in *Arts Reach*, August.

INDEX